GOD WITHIN US

GOD WITHIN US

BY RAOUL PLUS, S.J.

With a Prefatory Letter by

FATHER GERMAIN FOCH, S.J.

Done into English by

EDITH COWELL

P. J. KENEDY AND SONS
NEW YORK
1947

NIHIL OBSTAT:

INNOCENTIUS APAP, O.P.,
Censor deputatus.

IMPRIMATUR:

EDM. CAN. SURMONT,
Vicarius Generalis.

WESTMONASTERII,
die 30A Junii, 1924.

Lithographed in the United States of America

How many souls will one day utter a cry of surprise at the discovery of that *inner life* which is theirs, and of which they have hitherto been unaware !—MGR. D'HULST: *Lettres de Direction.*

THE AUTHOR'S GREETINGS TO HIS READERS

Omnis gloria filiae Regis ab intus.

"All the glory of the King's Daughter comes from within."

MAY the ever-blessed Virgin, to whom we dedicate these pages, grant to each soul who reads them the desire to penetrate into that interior castle of the soul which each one of us possesses, and in which, by his grace, God himself hath his dwelling.

PREFACE

Reverend and very dear Father,

   During the last four years we have prayed
without ceasing that war might end in victory.
Prayers, indeed, were needed. Victory was so
many times compromised, so often uncertain, so
frequently in the ba¹ance. Thanks be to God, the
victory of our armies is now beyond question.

   But God's victory—is that also assured ?

   " God's victory !" The phrase is not mine. It
was Judas Machabeus who found it, and made it a
watchword, and a battle-cry for his troops, when
he launched his attack against the Syrian armies.*

   France, England, Italy, America, and Belgium,
each had its " war aims." God, too, had his. He
would not have plunged the world into such disasters
without some great reason. What was his purpose ?

   First of all—as the Church implies in the Mass
pro tempore belli—it was that we might mend our
ways, and expiate our sins, both national and
individual. But that was not all.

   A few years before the war Pius X, on ascending
the pontifical throne, addressed to the world an
encyclical letter, in which he summed up, in four
words taken from St Paul, the whole object of his
pontificate. *Instaurare omnia in Christo.*†

* 2 Mach. xiii 15.   † Eph. i 10.

ix

There is no doubt that Pius X was the forerunner, the prophet, and the interpreter of the Divine Wisdom, and the will of God, during the years before war broke out; and that he was sent to tell us what God had in store for us, when he permitted this frightful calamity—the regeneration, in Christ, of France, and of the whole world, together with all that such regeneration implies.

And the events, the facts connected with the war—do they not show, better than any words could do, what great need the nations have of Christ, how much they have to gain by following in his footsteps, and how much to lose by failing to do so? Alas! " God's victory " is slow in coming! Is it even visible on the horizon?

The world was first born again by the Holy Ghost, on the day of Pentecost.

In order to bring about " God's victory " a second Pentecost is needed.

In order to bring about this second Pentecost, we must win God's heart, for with him nothing is impossible. *Quaecumque voluit, fecit.*

We shall win God's heart in proportion as we lay hold on the supernatural. It is a moral principle that like clings to like. God cannot fail to feel attraction and sympathy for the soul which lives after his divine life—which lives, that is to say, supernaturally. He cannot fail to grant the prayers of such a soul.

This brings me to my point—that it would be difficult to imagine anything in the supernatural life more concrete, and more striking, than the

mystery of " God within Us." It is this mystery
which you have put forth with such lucidity, and in
so convincing a manner, in this book of yours.

As often as the souls who put themselves under
your direction realize and make use of this means
of sanctification, so often will they be enabled to
taste and see, in their own spiritual lives, that which
St Paul claimed for himself and his disciples: God
maketh us to triumph in Jesus Christ*—*Gratias Deo
qui semper triumphat nos in Christo Jesu.*

Thus you will prepare " God's victory," by
spreading a devotion to Emmanuel—to *God within
Us.*

May the blessing of the Sacred Heart secure for
these pages the success they merit, that they may
broadcast the seeds of eternal life—that higher and
infinitely divine life which the Sacred Heart himself
constantly infuses within us: *Jugiter influit.*

I therefore send you, Reverend and very dear
Father, in pleasant remembrance of the many happy
hours we spent together in Holland,† my very best
wishes for the success of your excellent book.

GERMAIN FOCH, S.J.

MONTPELLIER,
   January 10, 1919.

* 2 Cor. ii 14.
† The author of the following pages had the benefit of
the spiritual direction of the Rev. Father Foch during his
three years of philosophy. They were years of exile from
France. Hence the allusion to Holland.

CONTENTS

xiii

GOD WITHIN US

BOOK I

OUR SUPERNATURAL PRIVILEGES

CHAPTER I

INTIMACY WITH GOD

THE end of piety, its object and reward, is *intimacy with God*. Comparatively few souls attain it. Many imagine it to be an impossibility.

What is the cause of this?

Chiefly, that we are in the habit of treating God as if he were *someone who is absent*.

How can we possibly be on intimate terms with someone who is never there? *Intimacy presupposes presence.*

Quite so. But can we, without indulging in a flight of imagination, treat God as if he were *someone really present?*

Among the different ways in which God is present amongst us, there is one which is, above all, a source of intimacy. It is that which we shall endeavour, in these pages, to describe, and, if possible, to make clear—the Presence of God within us, by the state of grace.

The catechism tells us that God is present *everywhere*. Some, but comparatively few, souls are impressed by a sense of this omnipresence of God. For the average man, on the other hand, a being who is everywhere is nowhere, and the majority of Christians fail to understand how an impersonal presence, difficult to conceive of, and existing alike for the sinner and the just, as a sole result of the act of creation, can possibly excite any feeling of intimacy.

God is omnipresent also, and in a special manner, *in heaven*. But heaven is so far away! It needs considerable mental powers to create a feeling of intimacy which will bridge over a gulf so great as this. It is all very well for St Thomas, whom his contemporaries describe as walking with his eyes for ever raised in divine contemplation; or for St Ignatius, whom Laynez compares with Moses, because he appeared to speak with God, face to face,* and who, says Fr. Nouet, loved, when he prayed, to be as near the roof as possible, in order to feel that he was nearer heaven.

God is also present in *the Eucharist*, and this presence, though still very mysterious, is much more palpable. We see something—feel something— something which guarantees his presence to our poor human nature. What we see, what we taste, are but the appearances. The reality escapes our perception. Nevertheless, what we do perceive supports our faith, so that, under the appearances, we adore the divine reality. But this eucharistic presence of God in Holy Communion lasts but a short while, nor can we make our lives one long visit to the Blessed Sacrament.

Besides these three ways in which God is present

* His favourite invocation was, as we know: *O Beata Trinitas!* and his constant prayer: *Oh, beloved Word of God!*

among us, there is another, which is, for our present purpose, much more truthful.

If we were to ask a child: Where is God? he would answer: In my heart. What causes God to be there? Grace. What can drive him from our hearts? Sin.

These child-like, but profoundly illuminating, replies sum up the whole of the doctrine on which, as I believe, we may build up a life of *intimacy with God*.

Nothing is more strange than the way we all have of passing by all that is most marvellous without giving it a thought. The moral beauty of religious devotion, the splendour of the Church, the dignity of the priesthood—who stops to realize what these things mean?

But we Christians do even worse. We are past-masters in the art of ignoring the splendid realities which lie *within us*.

Ask any baptized Christian what is meant by being in a state of grace. A state of grace, he will reply, consists in *not having* any mortal sin on the conscience. So far, so good—but, you ask him, is that all it means to him? Yes, he will say, and is it not enough? No, you reply. According to you, being in a state of grace means *not having* something. Does it not also imply *having something*? Having what? Listen, and I will tell you. It means that *God is present and dwells within us*.

This, neither more nor less, is the doctrine of the Church, and the teaching of the catechism.

God, then, is present, and dwells within us. We shall now proceed to show that—

1. Our Lord affirms it;
2. St Peter explains it;
3. St Paul makes it an habitual text of his epistles;

4. The Doctors of the Church vie with each other in preaching it;

5. The liturgy celebrates it in a thousand different ways; and

6. The saints lived in the contemplation of it.

How does it come to pass, then, that for the majority of Christians, and even of pious souls, this fundamental doctrine is practically a dead-letter—that this doctrine, which is the source of such great consolation, is either without weight, or absolutely unknown ? We can find a good many reasons for this strange state of affairs. First of all, we will point out one very good reason—that comparatively few people ever mention this doctrine.

" Reality," says Cardinal Mercier in a Retreat given to priests a few months before the war, " is God dwelling within us. Many baptized souls are ignorant of this mystery, and remain, their whole lives, unaware of it. . . . The very people whose mission it is to preach it throughout the world neglect it, forget it, and when it is brought home to them are astonished. Let me impress upon your minds the belief that God Almighty will never forsake you, unless, by mortal sin, you compel him to quit your souls. Make spontaneous, explicit, and frequent acts of faith in this real and constant presence of God within you. Seek him, not outside, but inside you, for there he dwells, calling you, expecting you, and grieving, because of your distractions and your forgetfulness."

In the writings of the learned Cornelius à Lapide we find the same regret. " Few men," he says, " adequately appreciate the gift of grace. Each soul ought to go down in respectful admiration before its presence within him; preachers and scholars should expound it and profoundly inculcate a knowledge of it in the minds of the people. Thus would the faithful learn that they are the living temples of the Holy Ghost; that they carry God himself in their hearts; and that it behoves them, in consequence, to walk divinely in his presence, and to live a life worthy of such a guest, who everywhere goes with them, and everywhere sees them." Mgr. de Ségur makes a similar complaint:

" All Christians know," he says, " vaguely, and in theory, that God dwells within their hearts; that they are the temples of Jesus Christ, and that the Holy Ghost abides with them. . . . How is it that so few people seem to attach any importance to it—that so few think of it, live in it, or have any practical belief at all in it ? I am not afraid to say that even among priests—good priests—there are but few who actually feed their flocks on this precious food for which alone they crave; which alone can satisfy their hunger and quench their thirst for God, the life of their souls, the treasure of their hearts, the companion of their lives, the intimate source of their strength, their sanctification, and their piety."

According to the *Message du Cœur de Jésus au Cœur du Prêtre* (found among the papers of a Marist Father who died in Rome, and probably communicated to him by some pious soul) our Lord has manifested a desire that devotion to the state of grace should be spread among the faithful.

" Devotion to my Sacred Heart has certainly spread rapidly. It consoles me, and is the means of bringing many souls to me, the Saviour of souls ! How little understood, nevertheless, are the infinite treasures of my heart ! Ah ! did they but guess how intense is my desire to unite myself intimately with *each* one of them ! Very few are they that attain to this union as completely as my heart has prepared it for them on earth ! And what is lacking to bring this to pass ?

" To gather together, and to pile up, as it were,

their affections, and to concentrate them on me, who
am there, in the inmost recesses of their souls!
Ah! cry out to them all how much I love them;
implore them to lend ear to the urgent appeal of
my heart, my tender invitation to descend *into the
depths of their souls*, there to unite themselves with
him who never leaves them; to identify themselves
with me, so to speak, and then—what blessings
will I not promise them!

" This mysterious and divine union will be the
beginning of a life which will be sanctified and
fruitful to a degree never before experienced by
them. . . .

" Many priests know well enough in theory the
meaning of this union of the soul with me, and some
aspire to it.   But how few know what it is in practice,
and how few, even among those pious and zealous
priests who are my devoted friends, know that I
dwell *there*, in the depths of their souls, all burning
with desire to make them *one* with me!

" Why is this ?   It is because they live, as it were,
on the surface of their souls.   Ah! if they would
only draw aside from the things of sense, from
human impressions, and descend thus *alone* to the
inmost corners of their souls, to their very depths,
where is my dwelling, how soon would they find me,
and what a life of union, light, and love would be
theirs." . . .

Mgr. de Ségur does not hesitate to take the blame
himself if the faithful fail to grasp this admirable
doctrine, which is nevertheless none other than
that which St Paul taught to the Colossians,* " the
mystery which hath been hidden from ages and
generations, but now is manifested to his saints,
to whom God would make known the riches of the
glory of this mystery."

* Col. i 26.

" We, the ministers of God," says this holy prelate, with his usual humour, "have not enough of the spirit of faith. We have the faith *in partibus*, like those good bishops who have no diocese. Alas! I also am one of these!"

It cannot be denied, however, that, for him who desires to be an apostle in the real sense of the word, it is first of all necessary that he should be able to appreciate the primary importance of this doctrine of the indwelling of the Holy Ghost in the souls of the faithful.

If we ourselves have not thoroughly explored it, by patient study and prolonged meditation, how can we be surprised if the faithful spend their lives in such amazing ignorance of the most precious treasure that exists, as long as this treasure is not deemed worthy of ardent investigation by those whose office it is to teach others?

Does anyone say that every priest who has done his treatise *de Gratia* has sufficiently studied this mystery, but that it is an impossibility to preach it, and to give it to the faithful, as food for their souls?

If this were true, it would mean that a fundamental doctrine of the Church, and that the basis on which rests the whole Christian life, must be ignored by the majority of Christians.

This cannot possibly be so.*

To whom does St Paul preach " the great mystery," the presence of God, by grace, within us?

It is to the curriers of Ephesus, and the dockers of Corinth—men no less " buried in matter" than

---

* " If any subject ought to interest us it is surely that; nothing affects us more personally; nothing is so precious to us, or more important. . . . The study of this mystery not only offers nothing to repel us, nothing dry, but it is calculated to stir us to the depths of gratitude, admiration, confidence, and love."—Fr. Froget, O.P.: *De l'Habitation du S. Esprit dans les Ames justes*, p. 184 (Lethielleux, 1898).

the average Christian to-day; men whose habits and whose pagan traditions must have made it harder for them to grasp its meaning than it ought to be for us, who are hereditary Christians, children and grandchildren of baptized souls.

Supposing, even, that we admit that all the faithful cannot benefit—at least in the same degree—by the idea of the divine Indwelling within us, may we not maintain, nevertheless, that many pious and fervent souls, thirsting for closer union with God, would profit considerably by having their attention drawn to this most important point ?

This, at least, is our opinion—hence these pages.

Many generous souls strive and strive again, and all in vain, to draw closer to God, because they do not turn, as they ought to turn in order to succeed, to this beautiful and fundamental doctrine, but seek rather to attain their end by indulging in sentiment, or by devotion to pious practices.*

In order to bring home to such souls the mistake they make, St Bernard bids them remember the story of St Mary Magdalen at the tomb:

"Many seek God where he is not—or rather, where he is not in a special manner. This is the explanation of all the confusion, all the lost time, and so much stamping of feet. ' Woman, thou weepest ? Whom seekest thou ? He whom thou seekest, thou dost possess. Dost thou not know ? Thou hast him, and thou weepest ? Thou dost seek him, but thou hast him within thee. Thou dost stand

* There is another difficulty—the danger lest they should confuse the divine Indwelling with certain unorthodox opinions which arise out of modernism, and which tend towards nothing less than the suppression of God, and the deification of man. We have already dealt with this question in the *Revue pratique d'Apologétique* (June 1 and 16, 1914) in article entitled " Notre Temps et l'Intelligence de l'État de Grâce."

by the tomb, weeping. Why? Where am I? I am *within* thee (*mens tua monumentum meum est*). There do I take my rest, not indeed dead, but living and immortal. Thyself art my garden. Thou hast well said, in calling me the gardener. I am the second Adam. To me also has been given the care of a Paradise. My task is to labour that there may spring up in this garden, which is thy soul, a harvest of desires. How? Thou hast me. Thou dost possess me, *within thee*, and thou dost not know it? (*Habes me intra te, et nescis?*) For this dost thou seek me outside. And behold, I am here. I did but appear to thee without, that I might lead thee within (*ut te intus reducam*). It is there, *within*, that thou wilt find me. . . . Ah, I am not absent, afar off, as thou dost think. I am very near. Tell me, what has anyone closer than his own heart? Those who find me will find me there, in their own hearts, for there is my dwelling. (*Illic intus invenior a quibuscumque invenior.*)' "

The object of the present writer is to set forth as clearly as possible (while at the same time avoiding anything which may possibly give rise to controversy) for the benefit of all pious souls who feel drawn to lead a truly Christ-like life, exactly what is meant by the Presence, or Indwelling of God within us.*

* For those who desire to approach the subject from a theological or patristic standpoint, or to gain information on any special point in connection with this matter, we will recommend, besides the works of Cornelius à Lapide (which will be inaccessible to the majority of our readers), Bellamy: *La Vie Surnaturelle ;* Fr. Nouet: *Le Chrétien dans ses Rapports avec la Très Sainte Trinité ;* Fr. Terrien: *La Grâce et la Gloire ;* Fr. Ramière: *La Divinisation du Chrétien ;* Fr. de Smet: *Notre Vie surnaturelle ;* Fr. Froget, O.P.: *De l'Habitation du Saint Esprit dans les Ames justes ;* Mgr. de Ségur (with certain differences which we shall point out): *Jésus vivant en nous ;* Fr. Foch: *Catéchisme de la Vie intérieure ;* Ch. Sauvé: *Élévations dogmatiques*, tome VI.

CHAPTER II

THE SUPERNATURAL ORDER

GOD did not create man with nothing more than a body and a soul.

The definition of man as " a reasoning animal " is philosophically, but not historically, correct.

Man, as God made him, and as God wished him to be, is more than a man. He is a man with *something superadded*.

Let us try to describe this *something*.

From the moment God wishes to create a being, he owes it to himself to give that being all that constitutes him in his own nature.

God wishes, for example, to create a tree. He owes it to himself to give it all that makes a tree a tree, and nothing more. If, however, having created it, God is pleased to endow it with some supplementary quality—say, for instance, with the faculty of moving from one place to another—this supplementary quality must not be looked upon as something appertaining to its nature, but as something beyond it—something supernatural. From the moment that God wishes to create an animal, he owes it to himself to endow it with all the necessary qualities of an animal. Need he do more? No. If, by chance, he does confer anything more, it is purely by an act of favour. If, for instance, he gives a horse, or a dog, the power of reasoning, this additional faculty may be said to surpass the nature of the horse or dog, and is thus, in the *literal* sense of the word, supernatural.*

* The difference between *supernatural* and *preternatural* is this: preternatural gifts raise the subject from a lower to a higher, but still *created* class; supernatural gifts raise him above *all* created nature.

So far, we have dealt with imaginary cases. Now we come to facts.

God wishes to create man. He owes it to him—or rather, to himself—to endow him with all that constitutes man's nature, and nothing more—a body and a soul, and that is all.

Revelation tells us that God, having created man, was, as if not satisfied by the result of his task, moved by a second loving impulse to add something to the wonderful gifts which constitute man's nature. Man has a body and a soul. It is enough. It constitutes the perfect nature of man. But *all of God* is not found there, in this his creature.

God has fulfilled his design, but he has not exhausted his love. He has not given enough to satisfy himself. He wishes to give something more. Man shall be not *only* man. He shall be body and soul—yes, and something far greater besides.

And God decides that man should be a participator in his own divine life.

Man will still be man; but, even on earth, he will be called upon to share the life of God, in order that, later, he may be able to do so more completely, and for all eternity, in heaven. His participation will still be partial, but direct, and the mystery will lie, not so much in the fact that man should be called upon to perform a divine action, as in this other fact, that he should be called upon to perform an action essentially divine (to see God face to face), and should nevertheless remain, in spite of it, a man.

These difficulties, however, are of small importance. I mean, of course, that they are important for the theologian, but not for those souls for whom this dogma is merely a source of piety. Moreover, the very difficulties themselves only serve to show how boundless has been God's love for us, his creatures.

Man was destined by God to give him thanks in a special manner.

God had attached to the possession of these splendid privileges (together with others, in the temporal order, and more tangible, such as freedom from suffering and death) the duty of faithfully observing his decrees.

By imposing such a condition on Adam, God was not acting contrary to his infinite goodness. He was rather giving him the opportunity of meriting— or appearing to merit—what was, on his part, a free gift.

But what happened ? Adam was disobedient, and all was lost.

As human beings what we feel most is the loss of the more perceptible benefits. Behold, now, from henceforth we are doomed to suffer—and to suffer horribly. And behold, we are now also subject to death !

The principal and only really essential thing is that all our divine treasures were taken away from us, and that, since God had united them to us so closely that their possession or non-possession meant life or death to us, the loss of them meant eternal punishment.

God, indeed, did not make first the natural in man, and then the supernatural. No. Both were created by the same act. Man was either to cherish for ever the treasures of divine life, and to see God face to face; or else, by banishing God from his soul, he was to see himself banished by God for all eternity.

Such was the law—and then man, wittingly, and in foolishness, preferred to forfeit the divine life. This is what is meant by original sin.

God will surely, as a punishment, leave man to his own devices.

Original sin—and, for that matter, all mortal sin too—means just this: that man chooses to be *only* man—*per peccatum, homo fit tantum homo,* as St Augustine puts it.   It means that man, the reasoning animal, rejects his divine gifts in order to satisfy his caprice; that he loses his greatest treasure —that which makes him, not merely the creature, but the friend, the child of God; that he is instantly deprived of the rich favours which, in this life and the next, were attached to the possession of that treasure.   We may well speak of *fallen man.*   It was a fall indeed.

Will God abandon man to this miserable state of being no longer anything but man?   Adam has wilfully refused his divine gifts.   Will God decree that the loss shall be eternal, and leave him, and those who will come after him, no hope of redemption?

We do not know God!   We do not know what great, what infinite mercy binds him to man, traitor as he was in Adam, uninteresting, insignificant and unworthy as he has been ever since, even in the case of the chosen people of the Old and New Testament, of the divine favour.

We are so accustomed to the idea of the Redemption that when Jesus Christ does not appear to us to be an altogether insignificant individual, of no account whatsoever, he seems to be just a normal being, not in any way remarkable, who came, one might almost say, to please himself, or to satisfy his own whim, and whose coming, therefore, is no reproach to us, but rather what we have a right to expect.

The supernatural seems to us quite natural. We do not see anything splendid and marvellous in the Redemption; neither do we realize that Jesus Christ is so amazingly different.   We do not understand that, if we did but pause to reflect for a single second, the work of our redemption by God himself would merit our endless admiration, and our constant thanksgiving.

We had lost all. God has given it all back. Yet the thought of it leaves us cold. Could indifference go further ?

There is certainly a difficulty.

If we have always seen a certain object, we cannot think that it can ever have been different. Which of us, as a child, has ever imagined that the scenes among which we were born could have been totally different—that instead of the banks of the Seine, or the Loire, it might have been the banks, say, of the Yellow River, or the Congo ?

In the supernatural order likewise, the situation in which we are born seems to us like so much scenery made to order in so many pieces, machine-made, and numbered, and made to fit together without any trouble !

But suppose for a moment that we had had no Redeemer—that the Redemption formed no part of the stock scenery ! It might very well have happened that, after the fall, no one had come to our aid. We might never have had a Jesus Christ. Once lost, we might have been lost for all eternity.

Lucifer sins—but there is no redemption for Lucifer. The bad angels rebel. God leaves them for ever to their fate. Why, then, did he save us ?

Like us, Lucifer and the bad angels had committed but a single sin. God does not save them, but he saves us. They were pure spirits, whereas we were of an inferior nature, having spirits clothed in bodies. Yet God saves us, and does not save the angels.

Yet, who pays the slightest attention to this ?

On us, the youngest of the family, God has mercy. On the elder members, who are bigger and more beautiful, and whose sin has been less heinous than ours, and the circumstances of whose fall were, at any rate, not so horribly childish, he has no mercy.

How dearly he must have loved us !

First he endows us with marvellous gifts—uncalled-for benefits, freely bestowed.   We lose these gifts—and God, who leaves others, and better than we, to their fate, has but one desire—to restore to us all that we have lost !

But what are they, these marvellous gifts ? What a magnificent treasure must this be, in God's eyes, that he should resolve that we shall receive them back, and at such a cost !

CHAPTER III

THE REDEMPTION

THE supernatural is, as we have seen, the divine life within us, which causes our finite nature to participate in the infinite nature of God.

Let us try to put this more clearly.   To begin with, we have at least one standard by which we can justly appreciate the wealth which has been bestowed on us.

Without knowing precisely of what my divine life consists, I can gain a fairly clear idea of it when I remember these facts: that God has redeemed us, and that Jesus Christ was made Man solely for this —that we might receive once more the supernatural gifts we had lost.

This tremendous step—that God should be made Man; that he should be born in a manger; that he should live among men, for thirty years a hidden, and for three years a public life; that he should die on the Cross—all this was but to one end: that we should become once more divine.   Let us meditate awhile on this.

As we have seen, we were, by Adam's sin, *tantum homo*, man, and no more.   But God will not accept this state of affairs.   His work has been spoilt, and he wants it unspoiled.   We have banished him from us, but he desires to return.

And the Word was made flesh.

St Ignatius invites us, in the *Exercises*, in contemplating the Incarnation, to penetrate into the divine councils, and to see the Holy Trinity deliberating on the fate of man, and on the means by which he can be saved from it.

Meditating on God, and his immense majesty, Taine compares man with an ant, and the Most High with an unconcerned individual who carelessly brushes aside with his coat the tiny object crawling at his feet.

How little Taine understood what God is!

Bending over man, the Blessed Trinity mourns his misery, and seeks a means of raising him from it.

You say that God is too great thus to humble himself?   But God is infinite goodness, and his tender love for man is infinite.

What is man, that God should be mindful of him, cries the Psalmist, contemplating with exaltation God's infinite tenderness towards man.

We are, indeed, profoundly insignificant creatures. But God's mercy is infinite.

What he would not do for the fallen angels, he will do for us.   The state of affairs is this: The crime which has been committed has been committed by a man.   Reparation, therefore, must likewise be made by a man.   Moreover, the injury done to God has an infinite value—and God alone can perform an action which will have an infinite value. Therefore, the Second Person, the Word, pronounces, in the highest heavens, the word of salvation. He will undertake the task of reparation. Son of God, he will become the Son of man. He will take upon him our nature, and become one of us. Like us, he will have a mother. He will lead a life like ours, and bear suffering such as ours. Reparation will then be made by man, because the Word will be made flesh. Reparation will likewise be made by God, because, in being made flesh, the Word will still remain the Word.

So the Incarnation is decided upon. The Saviour will become our brother by nature, in order that we may become his brothers by grace. He will share our life, that we may share his.

Such is God's plan. We will see how it is carried out.

The angel Gabriel appears to Mary, and speaks with her. God is seeking a mother. He has chosen her. Her consent is necessary. And Mary consents. She consents, and Jesus is born, the *Abbreviated Word*, as the Fathers of the Church put it—the miniature edition, made for our grasp, of the eternal Word.

God might have been content to offer us some formula of salvation, some rule which was to be observed. But we should not have understood. The Hebrews of the Old Testament had the Tables of the Law. But a charter is not enough to bind men, and the history of Israel is one long story of broken promises and betrayals.

The formula is a failure. The rule is never kept. Something more is needed. The Word will take flesh. Instead of following a charter, men will henceforth follow a man. The Son of God, who has become like unto us, will be our guide. He will be the elder Brother, of whom the whole family is so proud. Following in his footsteps, the younger ones will never lose their way.

He will show them the right path. *I am the Way*. He will ever be seen at the head of the column, and the two arms of the cross which he has chosen for his banner will shine through the dark, because, in their centre, there is a luminous heart.

Ego lux! Come, little ones—*filioli*—the way is rough, but I am with you. All I ask of you is to follow in my footsteps. Believe on my word. *I am the Truth*. He that hath been baptized, and will believe, shall be saved. He who will not hear me will be lost. . . . What, child, you have thrown down your burden of suffering, by the wayside? You are not following on? If any man would follow me, let him take up his cross, for thus, and thus only, may he come after me. . . .

Poor child! Your strength fails you. But strength shall be given you. At the moment of baptism the life of the Father descended upon your soul, and it rests with you to sustain and develop it. You have the means, they are my sacraments. If by chance you fall by the way, you must hasten to rise up again. Three times I fell on the road to Calvary, that I might, by the example of my courage in getting up after a physical fall, encourage you to get up after your moral falls.

I have given you an example, and more besides. I have put the means of strength within your grasp. You have confession, the most divine of all my sacraments, which I have given you that sin might not lie corrupting on your heart. As the Father might never have forgiven Adam his fall, so might I never have forgiven your sins. Dwell on this my goodness, not in order to abuse it, but to give yourself confidence. Every time you fall the priest will be there, ready and willing to give you absolution in my name. Whensoever, too, you suffer doubt

and depression, hear my priests. Hear the voice
of my Church.

Thus, I have given you an example, a rule, and
the means to help yourself. What more could
there be ? What could I do, that I have not done ?
And all, all, I have done, solely that you may share
the divine life of the Father, Son, and Holy Ghost—
that you may live a divine life. If I have done all
this, if I have taken such an enormous step—
sicut gigas—it is but in order that, as the Word, I
might make you participators in my life, which is
the life of the Father and the Holy Ghost.

Do you yet grasp a little of what this divine life
means ? No. You think nothing—or little—of it.

Yet, see what I have done. Try to understand
what it means.

Lord, I know. Increase my faith. Grant that
these great ideas may inspire my whole life. You
have rendered my life divine. From this day forth
I will meditate on this thought, and never will I
forget at what a cost you have done this for me.

Child, you have not yet understood. You have
but glanced at my life, and at all I have bestowed
on you. The manger was for you. My hidden life
was for you, and the gospel which I preached. My
church and her sacraments are for you. Have you
never caught a glimpse of the great shadow that lay
over all this—the dark, yet glimmering shadow of
the two rough-hewn limbs of the cross of Calvary ?

Earthly happiness might have been my portion,
but I did not desire it. *Blessed are the poor* was
the gospel I came to preach. Had riches been
mine, would you not have said to me: " Where is
your example ?" Therefore I chose poverty. At
Bethlehem I had nothing. On the Cross I had
nothing. During all the years between I had nothing. I might have been honoured, but I desired
to be able to say: *Blessed are they that are persecuted*

without incurring your reproach. Moreover, think on this: that no sooner was I born than one—Herod—sought my death, and more than once, when I was preaching, men would have seized me, and cast me into prison. They took up stones, to stone me. They returned my kindness with insults. As for the Passion—there were Annas, Caiphas, another Herod, Pilate, the jeering Jews. There was desertion, hatred, and treason. Nothing was spared me.

I might have—but I need say no more.

I chose suffering. I chose the Cross. I chose to give the last drop of my blood.

Why?

In order to bring home to you the inestimable value I place on that supernatural life for which your soul was made. I annihilated myself. I reduced myself to nothing, in order that God might dwell within you. I reduced myself to the *minimum* in order that you might reach the *maximum*. Alas! what bankruptcy, what failure has been my portion! All this I did for men, and how many men pay heed to it? How much do the majority of them care for the divine life which is —or might be—theirs? Sin is everywhere indulged in—in streets, in houses, upstairs and down, yes, and in the very churches, and the cloister. Above all, the sins of the good! For their sins I suffered the Agony in the Garden. For them I sweated blood. They were so many, so grievous, so heavy! I was crushed. I was overwhelmed.

I had given my life's-blood, and in vain. It was in vain, not only because there are a multitude of souls born without the faith, in pagan lands, but because of the thousands of souls—Christian souls—who betray me so thoughtlessly, and live in mortal sin.

He who first betrayed me, the unfortunate Judas, is the type and model of these souls who refuse to be

won. I tried by every means to touch his heart.
I tried kindness, compassion, threats. I went on
my knees before him. I washed his feet. He did
not understand. He would not take heed to my
voice. At last I could but leave him to his fate.

I gave my last drop of blood. Was it not enough?
To me it seemed enough, but man has baffled me.
Can it be thus that man's heart is made?

Turn your thoughts likewise to Mary, my sorrow-
ing Mother, who co-operated with me in the work
of your redemption, and in my sacrifice on the Cross.

She is also your Mother, not only because she bears
you a mother's love, but because, truly and indeed
(for such was my desire), you owe to her also your
supernatural life. What an amazing proposal,
what a strange compact Gabriel was to make, when
he appeared to Mary, at the moment of the Annunciation! "God," he says, "has resolved to
restore to man his divine life. In order that this
thing may be, he will be made Man, and he has
chosen you to be his Mother. If you consent, the
world will have a Saviour. If the world has a
Saviour, it will be saved. Without you, nothing
will be possible. You have but to give your consent,
and all will come to pass. But let there be no misunderstanding. These are the conditions: Jesus
will die on the Cross. You will rear him, that he
may be sacrificed. Without Calvary there can be
no Redemption. In order that the human race,
whose Mother, too, you will become (for the word
Fiat, falling from your lips, will give them supernatural life), may be saved, your First-born must be
delivered up. Do you consent? Shall One die,
that the rest may be saved?"

And Mary did consent.

She is my Mother, and you know, do you not? that
she is also yours, and that her true title, and that
which she holds most dear, because it best indicates

the part she has chosen, her vocation, her mission, is the Mater Dolorosa—the Mother of Sorrows.

All those years my Mother and yours had before her eyes the torturing spectacle of the Cross which overshadowed her life and mine. Every hour brought her the horrible vision of me, nailed bleeding for your sake to the Cross. For your sake, too, I permitted that this should be. Without this double crucifixion, mine at the age of thirty-three, and hers for a life-time, you would have had no redemption. With every breath that she drew Mary ratified the *Fiat* she uttered at the moment of the Annunciation. At the foot of the Cross she did but repeat with me, and after me, the ejaculatory prayer which filled her life—that sublime *Amen* with which she undertook to co-operate with me, with her whole heart, in the work of your redemption.

This, then, is the work of Jesus, and of Mary— to restore to mankind the supernatural life.* This is the debt which humanity owes them, and it is

* We do not claim that our Lady understood, from the first moment, the whole mystery of her Son's Passion, *in all its detail*. It seems probable, however, and such is the opinion of certain of the Fathers, that the Angel Gabriel disclosed to her the fact itself. Otherwise, how can we explain the note of resignation in her *Fiat*. If anyone makes us a proposal which will be altogether to our advantage, we say, not *Fiat*, but *so much the better!* Our Lady's humility, it is true, might account for her reply. But she had read the prophecies. She remembered the words of Isaias: *a worm and no man;* the *man of sorrows*. She knew that the garments of the Messiah would be stained with his blood. She understood that in consenting to be the mother of this Messiah she was consenting to be crucified with him, and that, for anyone who can read a mother's heart, means a mother crucified every day of her life. Mary was initiated into this sorrowful mystery at the first words of the angel. As far as the details are concerned, may we not suppose that, during the long years when he dwelt in closest communion with her at Nazareth, Jesus himself made known to her all that as Redeemer he would suffer?

precisely because she has bought us at such a great
price that Mary's prayers are so powerful with God
to defend us against the constant attacks of the
Evil One.

Because, unfortunately for us, it is not enough
that mankind should have been saved once and for
all. In how many different ways we are tempted
every day of our lives to fall into sin ! For each
and for all of us Mary is mindful of her task. She
delivered up her First-born for our salvation, that
we, her youngest-born, should escape death; and it
is on that account that her prayers are so efficacious
with God.

We read in the second book of Kings that the
mother of two sons lived to see the younger accused
of having slain the elder. He appears before the
judge, and is found guilty, and condemned to death.
But the mother flings herself at the feet of the judge.
" What, my lord," she cries, " I have already lost
one son, and you would take from me the one who
is left ?"

So we may picture Mary, *omnipotentia supplex*,
the all-powerful suppliant, crying out, when she sees
death, through sin, about to strike one of us her
children, and to deprive him for all eternity of the
inheritance which is his, as God's child. We may
picture her flinging herself at the Father's feet and
crying: " Lord, I delivered up my First-born, my
Primogenitus. In the name of all the pains he
endured, and of my pains also, have mercy on my
other son, on this one of my *others*. Be not angry
with him for ever. Grant him the grace of conversion. . . . Have mercy on me !"

Reader, do you begin to realize the value of the
supernatural life ? When you want to know the
value of a certain article, what do you do ? You
consult an expert.

I value my divine life at zero.

What value did the Blessed Virgin put on it ?

At how much did Jesus value it ?

Ah, they are experts, both of them, this Mother and her Son.   One of us three must be mistaken in our estimate.

Which of us is it ?

It is I who am mistaken. I must rectify my mistake, then, as soon as possible; and in order to do so, I must resolve, not merely to accept the opinion of another, but to learn, by personal experience, exactly what is meant by the supernatural life, and the presence of God within the soul which is in a state of grace.

BOOK II

THE DIVINE INDWELLING WITHIN OUR SOULS

SUCH, then, in broad outline, is God's plan for us:

In the beginning man, in addition to his nature, is overwhelmed with marvellous gifts, the greatest of which is the participation in the very life of the Holy Trinity.

This supernatural gift man loses, through original sin.

All is not lost, however, for God resolves to restore to man this ineffable gift. Certain other gifts, connected with it by a temporal nature, are, however, not to be restored.

In order that this restitution may be effected, God chooses himself to visit the earth. The Word, the Second Person of the Holy Trinity, is made flesh, the consent of the Blessed Virgin to be his Mother and share his sacrifice having been obtained.

Thanks to this work of redemption, we are once more divine. God has descended on earth solely to dwell once more within our souls. It was not the stable at Bethlehem that attracted him. It was our hearts. He desires to return to the possession of this kingdom, in order that we may be once more what we were originally intended to be—*God-bearers*.

We will now explain, in further detail, what this means. This will be no difficult task if we point out that, by sanctifying grace, God makes the soul:

(1) A real tabernacle;
(2) A heaven; and
(3) Another Christ.

CHAPTER I

"TEMPLUM DEI"

NOTHING is more frequently, and more insistently, repeated in the Epistles than this—that we ought to regard ourselves as *tabernacles*, as real churches, or houses of God—*quae domus sumus. Vos estis templum Dei.*

In support of his teaching, St Paul relied on the explicit doctrine of our Lord himself. "If any man love me," said the Master—and he means, if any man is faithful to his commands, and is in a state, not of mortal sin, but of grace—" my Father and I will love him, and we will abide in him, and make him our dwelling-place, our habitation, and our abode."

We will abide in him. Who? We—Father, Word, and Spirit, who are all one. We will *abide*, not in any general sense, but in a special manner, and out of love, so that he will be, not merely God's creature, the thing which he has made, but his friend.

We will abide in him. What a favour it would be, merely to come in passing, for a fleeting visit. But we will do more. We will come, and we will stay. We will come to abide, to dwell, to inhabit, in order that the divine life within the soul may be more and more perfectly fulfilled.

We will come, and we will stay. We will take
up our abode, and, as far as we are concerned, it
will be permanent. Our abode within the soul
will be *without end.* Man alone, by committing sin,
can put an end to it, and cause us to depart. Then,
indeed, we shall go; because we can no longer stay.
Until that happens, however, our presence, our life
within the soul, is a fact, a reality. Man has God's
word for it that this is so.

We are reminded here of the beautiful and significant words of St Paul, in which he points out
to the first Christians that as long as they are in
a state of grace they are, and will remain, " participators in the divine nature "—*divinae consortes
naturae.*

Let us try to realize what this means.

We have often meditated on the manger. Let
us try to imagine for a moment that it suddenly
becomes a living thing. In the cradle lies Jesus,
God made man. We, too, are so many cradles, and
within us hides, not the sacred Humanity, but the
Divinity of Christ. According to the symbolism
of the three Christmas Masses, the first com-
memorates the birth of the Word in eternity, in the
bosom of the Father; the second the birth in time
of the Saviour at Bethlehem; and the third the
spiritual birth of God in the soul of each one of us,
by sanctifying grace.

We have often meditated on the Holy Eucharist.
Let us imagine, for a moment, that the ciborium
suddenly springs to life. The ciborium contains
Jesus, God made man. By grace, each one of us
becomes a living ciborium, containing, not our
Lord's Humanity, but—greater far—his Divinity.

In 1914 some Belgian nuns, flying for their lives
before the advance of the German armies, took
refuge in Holland, bearing with them the ciborium,

which the Mother Superior had stopped to remove from the tabernacle. What deep joy must have filled the heart of that good nun at the thought of such a signal favour—that she should be permitted to carry with her God himself. But did she reflect that every day of her life, by sanctifying grace, she bore him, not indeed in the same manner, but in the most literal sense of the word?

Among the mentions in dispatches which we read of during the war, one of the most striking was that of a Basque from Urrugne, named Ururétagoyena. " Excellent soldier. . . . On June 16, 1916, during the burning of X, . . . he prevented the parish priest from going to fetch the Blessed Sacrament among the flames, going himself, in spite of the burning debris which fell on every side, and, getting through a window, brought it to the priest."

If this soldier was a practising Catholic—and, since he was a Basque, we may be sure of it—with what pride he must have carried, for those few minutes, the living God!

And we, too, how proud we ought to feel, if we only stopped to think that, *at every moment of our lives*, as long as we are in a state of grace, we are God-bearers. We bear him everywhere we go, not only *on* us, like that good nun and that excellent soldier, or like Pope Alexander, who always bore the Blessed Sacrament in a golden case hung round his neck, but *within our souls*, where he dwells, not in the flesh—this is a privilege we receive after Communion, for as long as the sacred elements remain with us—but *spiritually*, by sanctifying grace, as long as we desire his presence and are faithful to him.

We are *tabernacles*. The saints lived in this thought. As each year comes round we recite, in the breviary, the beautiful lessons for the feast of St Lucy.

" Is the Holy Spirit in thee ?" asks the prefect.

" Yes. Those who live chastely and piously are the temple of the Holy Ghost."*

We know, too, the reply of St Ignatius of Antioch, when the Emperor Trajan insulted him because he was a Christian, and therefore worthy of contempt.

" Let no man treat with contempt Ignatius, the God-bearer."

" God-bearer ? Why do you give yourself such a name ?"

" Because it is true. I bear God with me."

When occasion arises, our Lord takes it upon himself to remind certain privileged souls of the wonders of his presence in our souls.

" My beloved daughter, my temple, and my delight," he called St Angela.

St Gertrude, the saint specially devoted to the mystery of the divine Indwelling, the prayer for whose feast begins: *O God, who didst prepare for thyself in the heart of Gertrude a delicious abode*, heard the voice of our Lord, more than once, in these words: *I have chosen thee, that I might dwell in thee, and find in thee my delight.*

The knowledge which the divine Master wished to impart to these saints was not like that which we may all enjoy *by faith*, but rather knowledge gained *by experience*, and in a mystical manner, such as it is not our intention to dwell upon in this present volume. Having borne this difference in mind, however, we may still take the words he addresses to his saints to our own hearts. God can truly call each and every one of us his temple. To each and all of us, then, he may say, indeed and in truth: *I have chosen thee, that I might dwell in thee, and find in thee my delight.*

* *Estne in te Spiritus Sanctus ?—Caste et pie viventes templum sunt Spiritus Sancti* (Dec. 13).

For those of us who really have the gift of faith, this is no secret.

You will remember, perhaps, how Leonides, the father of Origen, used to bend over the child's cradle, and kiss him on the breast, because, as he told those who stood by: " I adore God present in the heart of this little baptized Christian." Later, Origen himself, writing on sanctifying grace, and the divine life it bestows on us, will use these words: *Scio animam meam inhabitatam. Habitata est quando plena est Deo, quando habet Christum et Spiritum sanctum.* My soul is a dwelling-place. Of whom ? Of God, of Christ, and the Holy Ghost.*

> Prenez garde à ce petit être;
> Il est bien grand, il contient Dieu.†

When Victor Hugo wrote those words, did he suspect that he was expressing one of the most fundamental and touching of the dogmas of the Catholic Church ?

I will remind you now of another story, similar to that of Leonides and even more beautiful, perhaps. A pious woman, after many years of childlessness, gives birth to a daughter. The child is put in her arms, that she may embrace it. " No," she says, " I will wait until she has been baptized." How many mothers have such ardent faith as this ?

No less edifying is the story told of the Breton poet, Botrel, who was summoned as a witness in a court of law, and, seeing no crucifix, refused to take the oath by raising his hand, but laid it on his breast, saying: " God, at all events, is *here*."

A certain French officer, who was sentenced to punishment in the fortress at Lille for refusing to act against his conscience in connection with the

* *In Jerem.*, Hom. viii.
† Cherish this little one. He is great indeed. He bears God within him.

persecution of the religious orders in France, used to console himself for not being able to visit our Lord in the Blessed Sacrament with the thought that, at least, nothing could prevent him from visiting God present, by grace, within his own soul. " To make a good act of adoration," he writes, " I enter within myself, or rather, I adore God present within me. *For are we not tabernacles ?"*

What a profound and striking thought this is, with those who are willing to accept what it means. In a letter written by Dr. Perié, president of the Aveyron branch of the *Jeunesse Catholique*, we read: " For my part, it seems to me that the whole Christian life hangs on fidelity to this maxim: to live every moment of our lives with Jesus Christ, and to feel him, God, the friend, the confidant, the Master, always present, by our side, and *within us.*"

What strength that thought brings, once we grasp its significance ! To be able to say to ourselves, every moment of our lives: I am not alone. I am *two*—he and I !

Let us take to ourselves, then, these words of Mgr. D'Hulst: " Let your soul be *a tabernacle* before which you often prostrate yourself, on account of the divine Guest who dwells within it."

CHAPTER II

"COELUM SUMUS"

" We are heaven."—St. Augustine.

Sister Elizabeth of the Holy Trinity, a Carmelite nun who died recently at Dijon, after only a few years of religious life, and whose piety was chiefly, if not exclusively, nourished by devotion to the mystery of the divine Indwelling within the soul, has left us a model of what a life of intimacy *within* may be.

Let none of my readers raise the objection that, in order to attain to such heights, we should all have to go and be Carmelites! As Fr. Foch very truly remarks, in a letter which is quoted in the beginning of the *Souvenirs* of Sister Elizabeth: " The specially attractive characteristic of this pious soul, and that which I appreciate most in her, lies in the fact that, when we have carefully analyzed the source of the virtues she practised, we find nothing but the expansion of grace, and the progressive, normal, and logical development of those theological virtues which have been bestowed *on each and all of us* at our baptism."

What does this mean? It means that the *sub-stratum* on which Sister Elizabeth's whole spiritual life was built is precisely that which we all possess. The divine Guest who was present within her soul abides likewise with us—for there are no two ways of being in a state of grace.

It is certainly true that the place each of us makes in his heart for God varies according to his individual capacity. This, however, is merely a question of *degree*.

Certainly, too, God can, and does, bestow special graces, which facilitate the spiritual life, on such souls as Sister Elizabeth. Yet, if we only have enough faith, how much we could all of us do to attain a solid grasp of this mystery of the divine Indwelling —for, when all is said and done, only two things are needed: good-will and practice.

That is why the *Notice* of this pious Carmelite may (with certain reservations which we shall point out) serve as a model for each and all of us. We intend, then, to borrow largely from it. So, you see, we go to St Paul for the theory, and for the practice to Sister Elizabeth, always bearing in mind that this practice must be modified in accordance with the circumstances and the exigences of the life each one of us is called upon to live.

We now have all the material we require, and can set to work.*

Sister Elizabeth herself tells us that the great secret was made known to her on the day when it dawned upon her that the words of our Lord, and of St Paul, regarding *God within us* were intended to be taken, not metaphorically, but literally.

God is within us—*i.e.*, the Father, Son, and Holy Ghost are within us. " The Three," as she calls them. She will listen to no talk of a far-away God. Her God is close to her. Her " Three " are all there, and her whole existence may be summed up in these few words: " intimacy *within*, with the Guests of my soul." From that day onwards her most precious thought (one, too, which we can each one of us share) was that her soul, which bore God within it, was a *heaven*.

We said just now that the soul which is in a state of grace was a tabernacle. We now see that it is equally true to say that it is *coelum*—a paradise.

" To live is to commune with God, from morning to night, and from night to morning. We bear him within us, and our life is an anticipated heaven," says Sister Elizabeth. " Grant that this ' God's house ' of ours may be all-invaded by ' the Three.' . . . It seems to me that this is the secret of holiness, and how simple it is ! To think that our

* We cannot refrain from referring the reader (again with the same proviso) to the *Notes Spirituelles* of the pious soul who writes under the name of *Marie de la Trinité*, and edited by us under the title: *Jusqu'aux sommets de l'union divines*. *Consummata* (Ap. de la Prière, 1921).

heaven is within us ! . . . How good it will be,
when the veil is drawn aside, and we shall enjoy
face to face." . . .

In a letter to her sister, she reminds her of these
words of the Apostle: " You are no longer guests,
or sojourners, but you are of the city of the saints,
and of the house of God."

" This heaven," she adds, " is in the inmost
recesses of our soul. Is not this a simple and a
consoling thought ? Come what may, in the midst
of all your cares as the mother of a family, you
can always withdraw to this solitude. . . . When
you are distracted by your numerous duties . . .
you can, if you will, refresh yourself, at any moment,
by descending to the depths of your soul, where the
divine Guest has his dwelling, and by meditating
on these beautiful words: *Your members are the
temple of the Holy Spirit, who dwelleth in you*
(1 Cor. iii 16); and on these words of the Divine
Master himself: *Dwell in me, and I in you*. It is
said of St Catherine of Siena, that although her
life was spent in the world, yet she dwelt continually
in her cell, because she lived in this interior habitation." . . .

The same thought dominates Sister Elizabeth's
Retreats : " My soul is a *heaven*," she writes, " in
which I live in expectation of the heavenly Jerusalem." And, finally, she sums up her whole life
in these simple but inspired words: " I have found
my heaven on earth, for heaven is God, and God
is in my soul."

Special graces were bestowed on this holy nun,
in order that she might penetrate more and more
deeply into this mystery. This facility for *turning
inwards*, and of " living alone with the One " to
the degree that was hers, can only be attained by
those on whom special graces have been lavished,

or who are, at the very least, preserved from the myriad distractions of a worldly life.

Our present purpose, however, is not to deal with such special cases. We do not maintain that everybody may enjoy the same privileges, but we do insist that God dwells in the heart of each and all of us by grace, and that it depends on ourselves (with the help of grace, of course, and in proportion to the opportunities each one has of living a life of piety) to withdraw, at the moment of prayer, *within ourselves*, because God dwells within us, and because nowhere else is he nearer to us.

Our blessed Lord deigned to explain this mystery, on one feast of the Ascension, to St Margaret Mary: " I have chosen thy soul," he tells her, " to be a heaven of repose on earth, and thy heart shall be a throne of delights to my divine love." This Presence, which is *felt* by the saints, can only be grasped *by faith* in our case. It is nevertheless one and the same, and the difference lies merely in the mode of perception.

This doctrine is often expounded by the Fathers: *Coelum es et in coelum ibis*, says Origen (*In Jer*. Hom. viii). Heaven thou art, and made for heaven. And St Augustine: *Portando Deum coeli, coelum sumus*. Bearing the God of heaven, we are heaven (In Ps. lxxxviii).

The *Imitation* echoes the same thought: *Ubi tu es, ibi coelum* (iii 59), which Fr. Faber translates: *God makes heaven wheresoever he is to be found*. This explains, too, why St Teresa used to fall into an ecstacy at the sight of a soul in a state of grace. " Heaven," she writes, " is not our Lord's only dwelling. He dwells also in the soul, which may be called another heaven."

In her *Foundations* and elsewhere St Teresa, like most writers in the past, dwells on this question of the presence of God within us from the mystical point of view. Occasionally, however, she recalls its theological and dogmatic basis. Adopting the phrase of Origen, *Tu coelum es*, she calls the soul " a little heaven . . . in which he who made heaven and earth hath his abode." " Is there anything so admirable," she repeats, " as to see him whose grandeur would fill a thousand worlds, hiding himself in such a tiny dwelling as our soul ?"

St Bernard, too, in treating of the soul, writes these words: " It must not only be called heavenly because of its origin. It must be called heaven itself " (*Puto non modo coelestem esse propter originem, sed caelum ipse posse non immerito appellari*).*

Now, in one sense, this heaven differs from that of eternity, inasmuch as we may lose it. Here below we carry our treasure *in vasis fictilibus*, but the other heaven cannot be lost. The heaven within our souls is invisible. God is present, but he is not perceptible to our senses. We realize his presence by faith, and not by vision.

In the Retreat she made before her first communion, Marie de la Bouillerie, who afterwards became a Sacred Heart nun, was struck by the words: " Our body is a veil which prevents us from seeing God." Between grace and glory there is only the space—so great, and yet so small—of this veil. At the moment of death the veil of flesh

---

* Again, he writes: *Non mirum si libenter habitet hoc coelum Dominus juxta illud Lucae : Regnum Dei intra vos est.* There is nothing to surprise us in the fact that God delights to dwell in our souls. As far as the visible heavens are concerned, he contented himself with creating them in a word; but for the heaven of our souls he fought, he shed his blood—*pugnavit ut acquireret, occubuit ut redimeret*. His task accomplished, delighting in his conquest, he said: *Haec requies mea, hic habitabo.* This is my rest; here will I dwell (*Serm.* xxvii *in cantica* No. 9).

will be withdrawn, like a cloak, and then—*we
shall see.*

Our treasure, then, is *liable to be lost;* it is *invisible,* and it is *beyond our perception.* Through
grace we possess it, but only in glory shall we truly
enjoy its possession.*

How much this means, if only we thought enough
about it !

I am heaven. And does it not also follow that it
is my duty to strive to make it *more and more true*—
that I may carry heaven *more and more* within my
soul ?

To sow eternity in time—is not that the sole
object of our existence here ? For what else did
we come into the world; and what man or woman
is there who, once having realized what this means,
would have any other object in life ?

* " At bottom," writes Mgr. Gay to the Abbé Perdrau,
" heaven is Jesus. It is not merely the sight of him which
is the soul's delight. It is the fact that he exists, and that
he belongs· to us. Now, he belongs to us here. The
definition of grace given us by the Angelic Doctor is therefore very true—*inchoatio vitae aeternae.* . . . We can,
and ought to, exclaim to each other in honour of God's glory,
and as a matter of mutual congratulation: *portio mea
Dominus* " (*Corresp.*, vol. ii, p. 247). It is well known
that Mgr. Gay had a particular devotion (which he constantly recommended to the souls under his care) to the
doctrine of the divine Indwelling. See, for instance,
Corresp., vol. i, pp. 247, 267, 284, 291, 316 ; vol. ii, pp. 8,
24, 39, etc.: *Instructions pour les Personnes du Monde,*
vol. ii (2nd edit., Paris: Oudin, 1894), two conferences,
pp. 61-108; *Retraite à l'Usage des Personnes consacrées à
Dieu.* Oudin, 1909.

CHAPTER III

"ALTER CHRISTUS"

To be a *tabernacle* and a *heaven* is the splendid privilege of every soul, so long as it is in a state of grace.

But we may go even further, and say that the Christian in whose soul God dwells is, in a literal sense, *alter Christus*—another Christ.

The Christian earns this title, first of all, by accepting Christ's teaching, and by professing it in the sight of men. For we must not forget that our faith should be something more than our private concern. Its rays should spread forth around us. It should be the badge or livery by which we may be known. *Induimini Christum. Put on Christ.*

Alas! how many baptized Christians are content to be neither more nor less than so many *sandwichmen*, bearing the name of Christians, and nothing more.

The Christian ought to be *alter Christus*, another Christ, because he ought, as far as in him lies, to live according to Christ's standards, and not according to the world's standards. *Hoc sentite in vobis quod et in Christo Jesu.*

But there is another, and even higher sense, in which the baptized Christian may become *alter Christus*. It is by striving to identify himself with him, in the most intimate manner possible.

What did St Paul mean when he wrote those words: *Vivo ego jam non ego, vivit vero in me Christus.* I live, but it is no longer I who live, but Christ who liveth in me? Many writers apply these words to the presence of our Lord within us, in Holy Communion. St Paul is referring, however, to the spiritual presence of Christ, as the Word, within our souls, by sanctifying grace. But because this thought, if taken literally, sounds almost too wonderful, many souls recoil from it, and, as if they were afraid, seek to soften down its significance—to coat it with sugar!

The best commentators have never pandered to this habit of dilution. Then take the words as they stand. " Why should we talk of imitation," asks Fr. Prat, " when the Apostle aims at mystical *identity ?*" We ought to resemble him not only because he took upon him our humanity, but because he has given our [individual] humanity a life like his own, and identical with it—the life of God himself."

As a Christian, then, I must wear Christ's livery. I must also live according to his standards. But, most of all, I must *identify* myself with him.

Christ shares the life of the Father. *Ego et Pater unum sumus—I and the Father are one.* We have here the divine formula on which our spiritual life must be based. The necessary modifications which affect our case, and which we shall not fail to point out to the reader, will not alter the substance. Christ dwells in the life of God. We dwell in Christ. Hence, by grace, we are participators in the life of God.

In explaining this mystery our Lord draws the following comparison: Behold the vine. The same sap circulates in the branches and in the trunk. The branches share the life of the trunk. I am the trunk. You are the branches. In me dwells the fulness of life divine. In you, in so far as you cling to me, is a share of the same life.*

* John xv 1-6. St Augustine lingers more than once on these words of our Lord. Among many others, we find this text: *Unius naturae sunt vitis et palmites. Propter quod, cum esset Deus, cujus naturae non sumus, factus est homo, ut*

St Paul chooses another illustration: Take a body and its members. The same blood, the very same life circulates in the body and in its members. The members have no life apart from the body. Separated from it, they are nothing. They wither up, and die. But as long as they remain attached to the body, the body gives them life and movement. Thus it is with Christ and his followers. Christ is the body. You, who are Christians, are the members. The life of Christ becomes your life, as since his life is life divine, so, too, is yours, because you are united to him. See to it, then, that you constantly remain members of Christ.*

We may picture the Father, Son, and Holy Ghost, the divine Trinity, as a boundless ocean.

By the mystery of God's infinite goodness, we behold this ocean confining itself within a finite capacity, a reservoir, vast indeed, but limited. This reservoir is the sacred Humanity of Christ. In him is contained the whole life of the Blessed Trinity.

The object of Baptism is to connect us up with this divine reservoir, which is Christ, in whom dwells the *pleroma*—the fulness—of life divine.†

A pipe which is connected with a reservoir by means of a running tap receives the same liquid as that which fills the reservoir. The only difference is the measure of liquid received, which varies with the capacity of the pipe.

---

in illo esset vitis natura humana, cujus et nos palmites esse possemus (tract. 80 *in Joan.*). And again: *Christus vitis non esset, nisi homo esset ; istam gratiam palmitibus non praeberet, nisi etiam Deus esset* (*Id.* Tract. 81).

* Eph. i 23.

† And that in two ways: first, by virtue of the *hypostatic union*, which is his unique privilege; and second, by possessing the maximum of sanctifying grace, a privilege which, thanks to him, we share with him.

At our Baptism we are connected up, as it were, with Christ, and from him we receive life divine. This life flows from him to us, and the *same life* circulates within us, as long as we remain in a state of grace. But let a mortal sin be committed, and the tap which connects us with the divine reservoir which is Christ will be turned off, and the Sacrament of Penance will be needed before it is turned on again, and we once more feel the divine life flowing into our souls.

This is but a crude comparison, but taking it on the whole it gives us, I think, a fairly clear idea of the way in which our life is bound up with God, *through Jesus Christ*. It explains, particularly, how, in order that God may dwell in us, it is sufficient that we should remain united with Christ. This is what we mean when we repeat, as we are never tired of repeating, at the end of all our liturgical prayers: *Per Dominum nostrum Jesum Christum.* In him we are participators of the divine nature, and no graces are bestowed on our souls save through him.

The example chosen by our Lord of the vine and its branches represents more faithfully what becomes of man when the sap of divine life no longer flows within him. He is a dead branch, devoid of sap—fuel for the fires of hell. If he dies in such a state, what is his fate ? Eternal damnation. *Aut vitis, aut ignis*, said the Fathers in plain, unvarnished language. Either we are united to the trunk, or else we are dead wood. There is no other alternative.

" The Christian," says St Augustine, " should fear nothing so much as being separated from the body of Christ. Once separated, he is, indeed, no longer a member; being no longer a member, he is no longer quickened by his Spirit; and whoever, says the Apostle, has not the Spirit of Jesus Christ, is not with him.*

One thing, then, is necessary—that we should not allow ourselves to be separated—that we should remain grafted, as St Paul puts it, on Christ. Thus will the life which circulates in him penetrate within us; and the life of Christ is none other but the life of God himself.†

But, although the same life dwells within Christ and within our soul, we perceive at once that certain distinctions have to be drawn:

He possesses it *entirely*, and we only *participate* in it.

He possesses it by *nature*, and we by *adoption*.

He possesses it by the fact of his *Incarnation*, and we by *Baptism*.

He cannot lose it; we, alas! may.

We shall find it more helpful, however, to insist not so much on such distinctions as on the resemblance between the divine life in our Lord, and in our souls; for the danger is not so much that we shall be too ready to think we are *other Christs* as that we fail sufficiently to realize the fact.

If anybody should feel tempted to take pride in this thought, or to exaggerate the presence of God within him, it should be enough to remind him of the words of St Bernard to one of his monks: *The ass which carried our Lord on his back did not cease to be an ass.*

* Tract. 27 *in Joan.*

† In order to avoid misunderstanding, it is better to avoid such expressions as: *Our Lord in us ; Jesus in us,* which are used by certain writers, and in particular by Mgr. de Ségur, in his very helpful little volumes. The words *Christ, Jesus, our Lord,* signify in the usual sense, the God made Man. By sanctifying grace the Son is within us, in the same way that the Father and the Holy Ghost are within us. He is present, that is to say, as the Word. In his sacred humanity, however, our Lord dwells with us only in Holy Communion, and for as long as the sacramental elements remain.

Creatures and finite beings that we are, the fact that we are participators in life divine does not make us God. It leaves us creatures. The Christian dogma of the divine Indwelling, rightly interpreted, has nothing whatsoever to do with pantheism. Those of us, moreover, who are in the habit of meditating on this mystery, know the magnitude of the task man undertakes when he makes the resolution that his life-story shall be " the prodigious poem of a poor man who tries to model himself on Christ." Far from being puffed-up with pride, we are confounded in humility. " The contemplation of the graces we have received makes us better understand our misery," as St Teresa puts it. " We tremble at being, as it were, a vessel which the over-weight of its contents causes to leak."

The fear, too, lest we should lose the divine Guest saps our self-confidence. " The impression which this thought makes on us is so great, that it causes us to walk with extreme caution, and to draw strength from our very weakness, that we may not lose by our own fault a single occasion to render ourselves more pleasing to God. The more we find ourselves overwhelmed with grace by the divine Master, the more we fear to offend him, and mistrust ourselves."

As far as the greater number of Christians are concerned, they suffer from anything but a tendency to make too much of the presence of God within our souls.

" Many Christians," observed Fr. Ramière sadly, " while they have faith in the divine promises, cannot make up their minds to accept them in all their magnificence. They are afraid, no doubt, to attribute too much goodness to him whose goodness, nevertheless, they proclaim. They persuade them-

selves that he exaggerated in making these promises.
Then they are told that they are called upon to
become the participators in the divine nature,
adopted brothers of Christ Jesus, members of his
body, and sons of the heavenly Father; to abide
henceforth with God, and eternally to enjoy his
happiness. The majority of souls look upon such
sayings as nothing but figures of speech, or pious
hyperbole.*

Eritis sicut dii. You shall be as gods, said
the serpent in the Garden of Eden—and it was a
lie. By sanctifying grace we become in very
truth " *filii Dei*—sons of God—divine men, other
Christs."

" I am the son of man and of woman, so I am
told," wrote a certain person. " It surprises me
to hear it. I thought I was more than that."

How many souls feel no surprise at all at hearing
it, and have no sort of suspicion that they are
" more than that "!

The dogma of the Presence or Indwelling of God
within us places all else in a right perspective.
In answer to those who may complain that by concentrating our minds on this mystery we run the
risk of losing sight of Jesus Christ, the historical
Christ, the man of Galilee, born at Bethlehem two
thousand years ago, we have but to remind them that
St Teresa, whose opinion is authoritative, used to
say that it was a matter of life-long regret to her
that at one time she gave up the practice of
meditating on the mystery of our Lord's sacred
Humanity.

Nothing has less foundation, indeed, than this
objection that rightly-conceived devotion to the
mystery of the divine Indwelling is calculated to
rob our Lord of his due place of honour in our
hearts. Devotion to *God within Us* in no wise

* *Divinisation du Chrétien*, p. 4.

excludes devotion to the sacred Humanity of our
Lord.

On the contrary, it includes it, presupposes it,
explains it, and sheds light on the whole story of the
life of our Lord upon earth. If the Word was made
flesh, was it for any other reason than that he might
return, together with the Father and the Holy
Ghost, to our souls, that we might once more become
participators in the life divine? *Societas vestra cum
Christo, in Deo.** As the Word Christ is, by the
same virtue as the Father and the Holy Spirit, the
efficient cause of our salvation. By the same virtue,
too, he dwells, as Word, within the justified soul.

As God made Man, he is the instrumental cause
of our redemption. That is to say, the blessed
instrument by which we have been bought back,
and through which we have received the Church,
the sacraments, and the means of salvation.

As God made Man, too, he is by his merits the
cause of our salvation—which means that we owe
life eternal to his vicarious sacrifice.

Finally, as God made Man, he is, by his example,
the cause of our redemption, inasmuch as he has
given us a divine model, which we have only to
gaze at, and to follow, in order to get grace here
below, and to earn eternal salvation.

Certain authors or commentators are too much
inclined to isolate our Lord. This is wrong. We
must incorporate the Saviour, the historical Christ,
with our whole supernatural history, and we must
always remember that Christ descended upon earth
for no other reason but to make us once more divine,
to reinstate the Holy Trinity in our souls, where
indeed it dwells, if we will but seek to find it.

There is no doubt that, for certain souls, the
contemplation of Christ as someone who lived a

* Osee ii 14.

long way off and a long time ago—the Christ, so to speak, of *history* and *geography*, is sufficient to bring him near them. They are able to picture the events of his life as happening in our own times, and in the midst of us. But this is merely a question of imagination. For the Christ who preached in Galilee *we* were present *then*, but as far as we are concerned the Christ of those days is not present among us. The Father, Son, and Holy Ghost, on the contrary, are in very truth present, and near us—within us—as long as we are in a state of grace.

What a far greater feeling of intimacy this thought gives us !* In order to speak with God, and to dwell with him, I have no need of imagination; I need not strive to transport my thoughts to those scenes in a far-off land two thousand years ago. No. Nothing is needed, save an act of faith. God is not far away. He is near me, *within* me—*intus*. I should be utterly devoid of intelligence if in such circumstances I were still incapable of feeling *close to* God.

CHAPTER IV

REALIZING OUR SUPERNATURAL PRIVILEGES

AMONG the private papers of the great Catholic scholar Ollé-Laprune, we find the following: " I am a Christian, by the grace of God. Do I really know what it means to be a Christian ? It is not enough to be a Christian merely by force of habit, or sentiment. I wish to be an enlightened Christian, from reflection, and by choice. I wish to ponder over this, and really to see what it means.

* For those souls, that is, who by diligent meditation on the mysteries of him who said, *I am the Way*, have begun to realize and to feel the need of leading a life with God.

I wish to bear in mind the fundamental principles of my religion, to meditate on them and examine them."

There are but few souls, indeed, who take their spiritual life as seriously as this; who are not content to take their faith for granted; but who feel a desire to realize what is meant by the supernatural gifts which are bestowed on all of us in Baptism.

If good Christians are not more Christ-like, it is solely because they have never realized their divine privileges.

God dwells within our souls by grace. For many of us, it is practically the same as if he were not there at all. *Realizing* consists in seeing that what we possess is in very deed and truth *actually there*. We are not called upon to *put it there*. All we have to do is to *discover* it to make it our own.

For how can the possession of such a treasure as this stimulate our spiritual life, if we are actually unaware of its existence ?

You may say: " I need not understand exactly what a state of grace means. All I need do is to see that I live in that state. I am not in mortal sin, and that is all that is required of me. It follows automatically, and without any need for me to understand all about it, that my life is meritorious, my conduct upright, and my soul pleasing to God.

As long as your standard is that of the average Christian, you are right. It is enough. But can we call the life led by the majority of Christians a Christian life? Of what does it consist, except of a certain number of pious practices, the real meaning of which is ignored? Of outward observance, and no more ! You can scarcely call that a *life*.

Si scires donum Dei. If we did but understand a little more, a little better, the gift of God ! If even we dimly suspected all it means to us !

Unfortunately, there is a considerable obstacle in the way of our comprehending this divine gift of ours. Like all supernatural truths, this great truth is something unseen, and invisible to the eye of sense, and it therefore runs a great risk of being completely ignored by most of us.

The first step we must take, then, is this: we must convince ourselves that these gifts are something quite real. They are there. It remains for us to make them our own. Let no one say: " I cannot feel anything, and therefore there is nothing there to feel !"

Many physical activities take place within us of which we are unconscious, as, for instance, digestion, assimilation, circulation. Why, then, should we be surprised to hear that the same thing holds good in the case of our souls ? We ought, on the contrary, to persuade ourselves that, in spite of the fact that it is beyond our perception, there does, indeed, exist another world far superior to that of sense.

God, invisible from all eternity, was once visible on earth, for thirty-three years. Can we say he only existed for thirty-three years ? He is no longer visible among us, yet does he not *live for ever* ?

The souls of the dead, when they have departed this world, do not cease to exist simply because they have been withdrawn from our sight and are no longer perceptible to our senses. When a man no longer has the power of speech, it does not follow that he is no longer able to think. It only means that he can no longer communicate his thoughts to us.

We live, then, not only in a material, but also in a spiritual world; and that which is more real is not the first, but the second.

And because this spiritual world is, in very truth, the only world which really matters, St Paul invites us to take it, and no other, into consideration.   Live, he says, not on earth, but in heaven: *Nostra conversatio in coelis est.*   Let your life be hidden with God—*vita abscondita in Deo.*   And again: *Invisibilia tanquam videns.*   Pay no regard, save to those things which are unseen.   The invisible world, however, does not mean the next world.   It means the world around us.   If, therefore, I am not going to resign myself to living half-asleep, and unconscious of the most beautiful and real world within my reach, I must accustom myself to regard the unseen as an undoubted and permanent fact.

Newman* insists continually on this idea, and sums it up in these two statements: Many things exist, and we know they exist, without realizing the fact.   Many words are heard by us which express a truth, known to us as such, and yet considered by us, because they are purely theoretical, to be practically null and void.

Let us take some examples.

Take the simple word, *hour.*   For those who have not *realized* its meaning, it stands for a mathematical total of sixty minutes.   For those who have realized its meaning it will mean (according to the mentality, the temperament, and the circumstances of the individual thinking subject) " the hour which passes . . . the passage of sixty short minutes. A minute—that means about a hundred deaths, and as many more births.   A hundred wails, and a

* See, in particular, his *Grammar of Assent*, of which, as a whole, it would be outside our present task to give an opinion.   See, too, an Oxford lecture entitled: *The Invisible World.*

hundred last sighs ! An hour—six thousand coffins, and six thousand cradles."

You see the difference, reader ?

Take another word: *cross*. For those who do not realize it, it means either a couple of pieces of wood, or else an algebraical sign. For those who do realize it, it will mean something like this: A cross was one day chosen as an instrument—a real cross, made of wood, was once put to use on a hill. . . . Once ! but to what a purpose ! Besides all the crosses upon which to-day there hangs the figure of our crucified Lord, there was once one cross, on which he hung, still alive, but nailed, bleeding, and dying for love of me. . . . How many words cease to have any particular meaning for us, because familiarity has worn them dull? Then, one day suddenly, and by accident, or as a reward for our efforts, they shine with a new brilliance, and become, as it were, charged with altogether unexpected significance.

St Ignatius observes that we should not glance rapidly at any truth we wish to bring home to our minds, but should pause, go back, and fix it in our thoughts—*gustare res interne*. It takes time, says Newman, to feel and to understand things as they really are, and we shall only learn gradually to do it.

If observation is so important when it is a question of concrete reality, how much more important and necessary it must needs be in the case of the unseen.

An idea—especially if it concerns a truth not perceptible to our senses—ought, in order to penetrate our minds, to resemble one of those pieces of wreckage which we sometimes see floating on the sea. For a long time it will appear to balance itself on the crest of the waves, until at last, out of the waves themselves, the sea-salt, some coral, or a piece of seaweed, will come and attach itself to the floating wood, and, little by little, it will begin to sink. . . .

Well, reader, that is just what *gustare res interne* means !

On the surface of our minds certain ideas are thrown, which float on it, without sinking in. If they are to penetrate, and become a part of us, they must gain weight by becoming attached, as it were, to a whole host of other ideas, which dwell beneath the surface of our minds—ideas which are the outcome of many memories, of our most precious thoughts, of our most delicate and penetrating feelings, and the sum-total of which will, as it were, attach itself to the new idea, and make of it something vital, and of practical use to us.

It is obvious that certain souls have more aptitude than others for this work of realizing the unseen. All of us, however, can reach the necessary minimum, if we do but exercise a spirit of faith. For note this—that we are dealing here only with what is within the grasp of all of us. God does, it is true, grant special favours to certain privileged souls.

St Margaret Mary was almost continually *sensibly aware* of the presence of our Lord. " Fix your eyes on your breast, and you will see," said his guardian angel to Blessed Henry Suso one day. And his body becoming, as it were, transparent, he saw God within him. " Thou art she who is not, and I am he who is," declared our Lord to St Catherine of Siena. " Contemplate me in the depths of thy heart, and thou shalt know that I am thy creator, and thou shalt be blessed."

Cases like these, however, in which it is a question of the bestowal of special favours, are outside the scope of the present work, which treats only of the presence of God within the soul, which arises from the fact that it is in a state of grace, and nothing beyond. And what is there to hinder any Christian whatsoever from applying himself, *by the exercise* *of faith*, to a discovery of the presence of God within his soul ?*

I go to church. Our Lord is there present in the tabernacle. I kneel down, and I say: " Jesus is there. He is truly present." And I proceed to develop my meditation.

I can do exactly the same, when it is a question of the presence of God within my own soul, by sanctifying grace.

" He began, as his custom was in mental prayer, by a deliberate act of self-exclusion from the world of sense. Under the image of sinking below the surface he forced himself downwards and inwards, till the peal of the organ, the shuffle of footsteps, the rigidity of the chair-back beneath his wrists—all seemed apart and external, and he was left a single person with a beating heart, an intellect that suggested image after image, and emotions that were too languid to stir themselves. Then he made his second descent, renounced all that he possessed and was, and became conscious that even the body was left behind, and that his mind and heart, awed by the Presence in which they found themselves, clung close and obedient to the will which was their lord and protector. . . . There he rested for a while. . . . He was in that secret place to which he had learnt the road by endless effort, in that strange region where realities are evident . . . and the Church and its mysteries are seen from within in a blaze of glory."†

* Certain writers make use of the expression: " to become conscious of God within us." This is not quite accurate, and is calculated to lead to misapprehension, for to *become conscious* implies *immediate* knowledge, and of the subject himself, whereas it is a question here of *mediate* knowledge, reached by means of reason and faith, and of the presence in the subject of *another* than the subject.

† R. H. Benson: *The Lord of the World* (p. 49). London, 1907.

God dwells within me. I believe. That is an *act of faith*. But the *spirit of faith* goes further. A man who exercises a spirit of faith is no longer content with a vague and more or less apathetic acknowledgement of a fact which appears to him to have no real significance. No. What was once a mere formula will become a vital truth, which will influence his whole life.

Is it expecting too much to ask every baptized person who wishes to make his faith a living thing, to say to himself from time to time, like Ollé-Laprune: " I am a Christian by the grace of God. . . . Do I know what it means to be a Christian ? Have I ever really thought about it ?"

" What strength and comfort we should derive from this conviction: God never leaves me. God is with me, and in me. He loves me. I am united, heart to heart, with his Christ. His spirit breathes within me, like the soft breeze of the prophet. I have only to listen, and to follow. I have only to recognize, and to taste. I have only to trust, and to hope. My life is no longer a stranger of whom it is my duty to take leave, in order to follow in the Master's train. He himself adopts it, and makes it his own, in making me his. I walk hand in hand, between my life and my Master, turning my back on nothing but sin, avoiding only what is less good; and the presence of the Celestial Friend, so far from distracting my attention from the daily round, will inspire me to apply myself to it, gladly and steadily, for what is my work is also his."*

Is it not this, in very truth, that makes man great —this fact that God is pleased to abide with ever-increasing fulness in his soul ?

* Sertillanges: *La Vie en Présence de Dieu* (p. 550), *Revue des Jeunes*, May 10, 1918. See also the same, March 10, 1919: *La Vie de Silence*.

We are sometimes surprised, and even frightened, when we reflect to what an extent everything in present-day society—government, public services, administration, and so forth—has been secularized —so much so, indeed, that if peradventure any-one should ask: What difference would it make to the world if the supernatural did not exist, if the Redemption and the Sacrifice of Calvary were nothing but a dream, and Jesus Christ simply a mythical personage ? we should hardly know how to reply, or, rather, we should be forced to admit that, as a matter of fact, it would make little or no difference at all.

The responsibility for this state of affairs falls on a good many shoulders. A large share of it, how-ever, falls on us Christians, who, possessing as we do such splendid and magnificent gifts, forget to make use of them. Ozanam, writing in 1834, makes the following complaint:

" I have felt that, up till now, although I have never given up pious practices, I have never suffi-ciently taken to heart the thought of that real world which is invisible."

It was humility which prompted these words in the case of Ozanam. In our case, how do we stand in this matter ?

The time has come when we should begin to realize our divine privileges: " The inner life, by grace, with Jesus. Soul, thou art not alone. He who makes thee divine abides with thee. Thou hast been *naturalized divine*." These are the words of a convert. It often happens that converts see more clearly than we others, who are born in the faith, for the reason that what we take as a matter of course is to them a source of wonder and delight.

" The magnificence of the humblest soul, in the wretchedest and most poorly-clad body !" con-tinues Loewengard. " The magnificence of this soul touched by grace ! It becomes an immortal palace, wherein dwells the King of kings, the Lord of lords, God in three Persons.

" Is it possible ? Is it credible ? Can the soul which is in a state of grace actually possess the Trinity, and *know* [he says *feel*] him to be present in his spirit and in his flesh, and love it as a bride loves her bridegroom ?

" Oh, if man is infinitely vile in the flesh, which is but earthly clay . . . he is yet infinitely strong, and infinitely noble, inasmuch as, by grace, he participates in the divine life !"

Why, then, should man be so ready to belittle himself ? Why, being so great, should he be content to lead such a petty existence ?

What a grave sin of omission, what gross contempt for the most elementary idea of the supernatural prompts men deliberately to organize society without the smallest regard for anything but their material benefit ! How terrible a thing it is that we, for our part, should be content practically to ignore man's greatness—man, such as God made him, with, not merely a body and a soul, but (to borrow the beautiful, but not always rightly-interpreted words of Tertullian) " body, soul, and Holy Ghost."

What pride, and, at the same time, what humiliation, to regard man as just man—and nothing more !

We have been *naturalized divine*. We have, then, no longer any right to behave as aliens, and we have no right at all to be either active or passive spectators of the betrayal of a society which, like ourselves as individuals, owes allegiance to God.

There is a tendency more and more to banish God, to ignore him and to induce men to regard themselves as human beings, and nothing more. To put pressure on nations or individuals to neglect or deny the supernatural is to seduce them from their allegiance, and set them on the path to that place of eternal punishment which will be the abode of traitors who have forfeited their naturalization— the place where, in accordance with the wishes of an impious people, God is nowhere to be sought.

Briefly, it amounts to this: We are Sons of God. It ill becomes us to behave as if we were but vulgar sons of men. We should live divinely, and do all that in us lies to help those around us to do the same.

Let us try, then, more and more to realize our supernatural privileges, and to help others to understand, that henceforth they may walk as becomes *God-bearers*.

It has been truly said that the pagan world would have been more attracted towards Christianity if its more characteristic features, instead of being kept in the background, had been held up to view, that all might enjoy their strange but splendid vision.

In speaking of our supernatural gifts, Fr. Gratry wrote these words: " If all this is true, how is it that men pay so little attention to it ? True, men are accustomed to move among much that is marvellous, without as much as a suspicion of the fact. And is not the presence of God within our hearts the greatest of all marvels ? Yet who has any suspicion of it ? Who cares anything at all about it ? Say nothing to them, said Fénélon, for they see nothing and think nothing."[*]

Yet, " *Life with the divine Guest of the heart* is a normal state, and one which every baptized soul ought to be leading. Alas ! what are the facts ? One in a thousand—one in ten thousand, perhaps, correspond to this gift of God !"[†]

[*] *La Philosophie du Credo*, p. 220.
[†] Mgr. de Ségur: *Le Chrétien vivant en Jesus*, p. 289.

Is not this a heart-breaking state of affairs, and ought we not to put a stop to it ?   And, indeed, what hinders us, as far as we, personally, are concerned, from living the normal life of baptized Christians, and from corresponding diligently to *the gift of God* ?

BOOK III

MORTAL SIN, AND RUPTURE WITH GOD WITHIN OUR SOULS

ONE of the ways which will help us to realize our supernatural privileges is the thought of what becomes of us, when, by mortal sin, we turn our back on these privileges, and cast them away, like so many useless incumbrances. Up to the present we have been considering the fact of the divine Indwelling from a *positive* standpoint. We have seen what it *is*. We must now consider the same fact from a *negative* standpoint. We must find out, that is, what it means *not* to possess it. God—Father, Son, and Holy Ghost—dwell within our souls by sanctifying grace.

Let us now consider what will be the effect of mortal sin on our relations with—

(1) The Father;
(2) The Son;
(3) The Holy Ghost.

When we have done this we shall have advanced one more step in the study of the adorable mystery on which we are now engaged.

CHAPTER I

WITH GOD THE FATHER

A CERTAIN wealthy man met a poor child in the street, and took him by the hand and adopted him. He brought him up, fed him, and surrounded him with every care. The child has his place at the family table, and shares in the family feasts. He enjoys all the privileges and the advantages which his position as a member of the family, a " King's son," entails. Later on, if he remains faithful, his adopted father will give him a share in the family inheritance. On one condition, however—that he should not leave home, or betray the person or the interests of him who has taken him in, brought him up, and raised him to his present high position.

The child grows up and becomes a man, and allows himself to be persuaded to abandon his adopted father, to renounce his privileges and his promised inheritance. Or, worse still, he tries to make away with the father, and to step in his shoes, that he may be master in his stead.

His plans go astray, and what is the result ? The father keeps his titles, and influence, and fortune, and the child finds himself banished for ever from what was once his home.

" Out of my sight," cries the father, " for I no longer own you as my child !"

This is a very good illustration of what theologians call *divine adoption*, and of the way in which man has rewarded the Most High for having made him, out of love for him, his adopted son.

In the beginning God was pleased to raise man to a supernatural height, and freely to superadd wonderfully to his natural gifts, promising him that, if he is faithful, he shall enjoy heaven hereafter, while here below likewise he will enjoy divine favours. Man, however, duped by the devil, with his lying promise: *Eritis sicut dii*, aspires to dethrone God, preferring his own caprices to obedience. For his misdeeds man forfeits his earthly paradise, and is deprived of his divine gifts.

We read the following anecdote in the *Simples Histoires* of Mgr. de Ségur:

A father loses his daughter in the middle of a fair. He searches long for her, but all in vain. Four years later he goes to London in the hope of tracing her, and comes on a girl, upon the platform of a boxer's tent. It is his daughter. He climbs on to the platform. " My child !" he cries. But the little girl, who has forgotten the days of her infancy, and has doubtless been spoilt by the vagabond life she has led since, and contaminated by bad company, replies: " You my father ? I don't know you. That is my real father "—and she points to the sinister-looking mountebank who has hastened to the spot to prevent the rescue of his victim.

How often does man, attracted by unwholesome curiosity and cheap joys, duped by the devil, the robber of souls, let go his Father's hand ? The wretched creature to whom he falls a victim drags him down, and carries him afar off. He tries to avoid the eye of God, which searches for him. God, indeed, knows well enough where he is to be found, only, when he knocks at the door of his heart, and appeals to him, either by remorse, or by the voice of the priest, the demon redoubles his efforts, brings out all his bag of glittering baubles, attracts his whole attention, and paralyzes his will.

If only, when we turned our backs on God, it was for something better worth our while !

But no ! The merest trifle is sufficient to attract us. We sell ourselves for nothing—for a glance, a book, a word, a fancy. What, says St Augustine to the sinner, you suffice to God, and does not God suffice you ? You go without, in search of what is nothing ? Seek rather within thee the sovereign good.

Within you. That is just what makes it all the worse. To sin against someone who lives at a distance is bad enough, but to sin against someone who actually lives with us, and whose life is most intimately bound up with our own, is not only unworthy and dishonourable to the last degree, but it means that we can have no love for him in our hearts.

The child who was kidnapped at the fair was hardly responsible. She had scarcely learnt to know her own father. But what about us ? Can we make the excuse that God is unknown to us ? Can we say, either, that he has ever been lacking in kindness ?

No sooner has a soul escaped from his hands, than God sets out without delay in search of him who would avoid him. He tries every means, every inducement. He knows only too well what miserable embraces, what sordid pleasures we are tasting, and he hovers round us in our misery, waiting for the moment of our repentance, standing with arms outstretched, and appealing to us by outward signs and inward prayers. " My child," he entreats, " it is I. It is thy kind Father. Return, I implore thee. If thou didst but know how greatly I desire to make thee once more my own."

What a splendid pendant to the story of the Prodigal Son, and of the steps he takes to return to his father, is this other story of the father, and the steps he takes to recover his daughter. Yet it but dimly reflects the loving-kindness of the Father who seeks after the soul that would avoid his embrace.

We can find no better example of this loving-kindness of the all-merciful Father than the story of his dealings with his chosen people. We find them constantly flying from his advances, while he endeavours by every means—by warning and by entreaty—to bring them back to their duty. Some-times—but how rarely !—the Israelites understand. More often they persist in their sins, or else, once having repented, they fall again and again, and turn a deaf ear to the voice of God and his prophets. What sorrow—what disgust, even—must God have felt, to see how little his chosen people were pre-pared to do him service, so that, finally, and, as it were, worn-out, he passes judgement on them: " It is enough, O Israel. Heretofore have I called thee my people. Henceforth thou art no longer my people."

We turn over the pages, expecting to find that God's anger has shattered Israel. Instead, what do we find ? We find God repenting of his anger ! The Israelites make a pretence of turning from the error of their ways, and behold ! God has not the heart to carry out his threats ! He cannot bring himself to refuse to forgive his children !

And if this happens once in the history of the chosen people, it happens ten, twenty times—in fact, *every time !*

Our Lord makes use of a number of comparisons to bring home to us the loving solicitude with which the Father of mankind sets out to recover the child who has been alienated from him by sin.

First there is the housewife who loses a piece of money. What a thorough search she makes for it ! She lights her lamp, looks underneath all the furniture, and sweeps every corner. Then there is the shepherd who loses one of his lambs. See how he sets out to find it, looking behind every bush, asking every passer-by, following every track, walking by every precipice, dropping with fatigue, but refusing to give up, until at last he comes upon it, under a lonely rock, starving and dying of fright. And then, how joyfully he calls that foolish lamb by its name, and, picking it up, puts it on his shoulder and brings it back to the fold !

His joy is so great that, in order to describe it, our Lord uses the strongest language. " There is more joy in heaven," he says, " over one sinner that repenteth, than over ninety-nine just that need no repentance."

During a certain mission, after a sermon on the parable of the Good Shepherd, a working-man went to the preacher, and asked him to hear his confession.

" It's that story of the shepherd going to find his sheep that was lost. . . . I said to myself ' I'm just like that sheep.' "

Yes—and we can all say the same. We are all of us " just like that sheep."

CHAPTER II

WITH GOD THE SON

Towards God the Father mortal sin is an act of the blackest ingratitude.

Towards our Lord it is an act of *treachery*, and *perjury*. The neglect to fulfil an engagement, the wilful violation of a treaty, either between one nation and another, or between State and Church, or between man and God, is none other than the same felony.

Now, it cannot be denied that we have all of us undertaken to fulfil the most solemn and the most sacred obligations towards our Lord.

Did we not, on the day of our first communion, declare that we would renounce Satan, and follow Christ ? For how long did we promise to do this ? Was it for a day, a week, a year, twenty years, or until we got married ? No. We promised to follow him *ever*. For *ever*—that means until the day of our death, and for all eternity.

For a time we kept our promise.

The day comes, however, when we are violently tempted. We give way. We commit mortal sin.

It is once more a case of a " scrap of paper " !

We had made a mutual compact with God, and now, who repudiates that compact ? " I will renounce Satan, and follow after Christ." That is what we said; now we say the opposite: " I will renounce Christ, and follow after Satan. I will have no more to do with Jesus. I deny him. Satan shall be my master, from this day forth."

I do not mean, of course, that—except in cases of extraordinary malice—we say this to ourselves in so many words. No. But that is what it amounts to, when we commit mortal sin. We are given the choice between Christ and his adversary—and we choose Satan.

Think what it means to be summoned to answer a charge of high treason at God's tribunal.

When the order is given for the general mobilization of consciences; when every human being, living or dead, is called up; and when the dread word is passed: *Arise, you dead*, what terror will strike the hearts of those of us whose consciences accuse us of having played the coward.

Every deliberate and unabsolved sin which we have committed will meet with its reward: "Christian, by your own act you have forfeited your rank. Your will be done. *Fiat voluntas tua, homo, in aeternum.* You put me far from you. So be it, and for all eternity. And now, do you disappear from my sight. I know you no longer. You have torn off the badge of your service. Henceforth you will walk alone, whereas you and I might have marched shoulder to shoulder. Remain as you are. Keep what you have. I will depart from you, or rather, I will remain afar off, even as you desired!"

It was the custom in the early Christian Church to clothe the neophyte in a white robe, which he wore for eight days after his reception into the Church, in order to remind him of the pledges he made at his baptism. We have a relic of this custom in the baptismal service to-day, when the priest places his white stole on the head of the infant, and pronounces the following words: *Accipe vestem candidam quam immaculatam perferas ante tribunal D. N. Jesu Christi.* Receive the garment of innocence, and see to it that thou dost give it back without spot—immaculate—at God's tribunal.

The white dress, or armlet, which we wear at our first communion has the same significance.

What have we done to redeem these solemn promises? Then, our garment was without spot. Have we kept it so?

At the time of the cruel persecutions by the Vandals, an apostate named Elpidophorus was consumed with hatred for a certain deacon who had remained faithful. This deacon, whom the conduct of Elpidophorus hurt to the quick, obtained possession of the garment in which he had clad the apostate on the day of his reception into the Church, and laid wait for him. When Elpidophorus came in sight, he shook out the white robe, and held it before him like a standard. "Behold," he said, "this white robe. You will recognize it. To-day you profane it. It will bear witness against you at the day of judgement. Take heed to your ways."

It is not even as if he whom we betrayed with such criminal thoughtlessness were nothing more to us than simply an individual to whom we had pledged our word.

No. All we are, we owe to him, and what sufferings he willingly endured in order to make us what we are! We know what was the price of our Redemption, and what were the tortures it involved. The sorrows of Christ, his pains, the blood he shed for us, the horrors of his Passion—all this is made fruitless by our sins. More than that, we can say truly that every time we fall into sin we renew his awful Passion. The real executioners of Christ are not the Roman soldiers who turned up their sleeves, the better to belabour his shoulders, to spit in his face, and to clothe him in purple in the guardroom at the Antonia fortress; or who nailed his hands and feet, and struck his thorn-crowned head on Mount Calvary. No. It is we ourselves who are indeed his executioners.

In a certain parish church the large mission crucifix showed signs of coming to pieces. The priest sent for a man to fasten the nails which held our Lord's body to the cross. The man gets a ladder, climbs it, and suddenly, finding himself face to face with the figure of his crucified Lord, is seized with regret. For a long time he has not been to his duties, but now his faith stirs within him. Repentance fills his heart, tears spring to his eyes, and the hand which wields the hammer falls to his side. "Father," he whispers to the priest who is standing by the ladder, "I can't do it. I tell you, I can't!"

If only the thought of our Lord's sufferings could be brought home to us as vividly as that in moments of temptation, how much less easily we should fall into sin!

In a very ancient life of St Dominic we find the following story:

A woman of more than doubtful reputation finds herself, for a wonder, alone in her house one evening. Suddenly, she hears a knock. She opens the door, and sees a strikingly handsome man standing there, apparently in great distress. She invites him to share her meal. He accepts, and sits down—and she notices that the tablecloth in front of him is stained with blood. She hastens to change it, and to spread a fair white cloth before him. A few seconds later, this too is stained with blood.

Then she understands. It is no mortal man who sits at her table. It is the Man of Sorrows, who was crucified on Calvary. Moreover, this blood which has been shed—yes, she knows, it is the price of her sins.

Is this a true story? It matters very little. In any case, its symbolism is just.

All mortal sin is *treachery* and *cruelty* to our Lord.

CHAPTER III

WITH THE HOLY GHOST

THE sacrament which makes us children of God, and which makes possible the divine Indwelling within our souls, is the sacrament of baptism.

We should realize better the presence of the Holy Trinity within us, by grace, if we meditated from time to time on each one of the sacraments which unite us with Christ.

We have already dwelt on some very significant words in the baptismal service. There are others which will provide us ample food for wholesome reflection.

The little child is brought to be baptized. He may not yet enter the church. He must wait on the threshold, for he is still " outside the Church."

The priest asks certain questions, and the sponsors give proof, on behalf of the child, of the formal desire of the future " son of God."

The touching ceremony proceeds.

" Wilt thou be baptized ?" " I will." And so on.

The priest continues, and no words, save the words on consecration in Holy Mass, reveal better than these the incomparable power of the priesthood.

With what assurance, what absolute certainty of being obeyed, this man in his cotta and stole speaks. His words are addressed to the demon. Depart, he says, unclean spirit. Depart from this child, and give place to the Holy Spirit. *Exi ab eo, immunde spiritus, et da locum Spiritui Sancto*.

What a touching parallel ! Someone is in possession of the soul of this tiny infant, by the fact of original sin. Who is it ? It is Satan, the Evil One. But the term is not sufficiently contemptuous. He must be called here, and publicly, by the name which best describes his activities. Nor does the Liturgy shrink from uttering it. " Depart, *unclean* spirit—*immunde spiritus*—vile and filthy spirit. Depart, and make way—for whom ? For the *Holy* Spirit !

And immediately, by virtue of these divine words, Satan flees, and the Holy Spirit comes to dwell for ever—as far as he is concerned—in the soul of the newly-baptized Christian. *Veniemus et mansionem apud eum faciemus.* " We will come —and we will stay !"

St Louis loved to sign himself *Louis de Poissy*, after the place where he received the sacrament by which he had been made a Christian, and which had caused the Holy Spirit to take possession of his soul.

Ought we not to follow his example—to train our minds to linger lovingly on the sacrament of our baptism ? The devil does not forget it. He left our soul, at the priest's command, but not without looking back. He went because he had no choice in the matter. The order was categorical, and not to be questioned. He fled—but, as soon as possible, he will return.

The Holy Spirit now reigns supreme in the soul of the child; but Satan will give himself no peace until, with the connivance of him whom he has been compelled to abandon, he shall be re-established in the domicile which he regards as his own property. He cannot attack God in his sovereign Person, but he can attack him in his *possessions*, and his greatest ambition is to expel the Holy Spirit from the heart of man, and to dethrone him, in order that he, in his turn, may take possession of our souls, and reign there, supreme.

What is at stake in this struggle between God and Satan ? Nothing more or less than our supernatural privileges—the life of God within us.

Let us glance at what the devil has to offer us, in exchange for what he takes away.

When he thought to lead the Son of Man himself into temptation he set him, the gospel tells us, on a high mountain, and there, with a sweep of the arm, showed him the whole world at his feet. " All this," he says, " is yours, if, falling down, you will adore me."

And mark, that it is not to Christ only that these seductive proposals are made. In order to get possession of *any* soul (or, rather, of the treasures it possesses) Satan declares himself ready to offer us in exchange every sort of material benefit. Of course. There is no comparison. The devil cannot fail to get the best of the bargain.*

Let us suppose for a moment that the devil is successful. *Si cadens* . . . All sin means a *fall*. The soul falls, and grievously. Apparently, however, nothing has happened. Of two people who meet in the street one is in a state of grace, and the other is in mortal sin. Can anyone see any difference between them ? No. Nevertheless, what a difference indeed there is !

In the hidden but real fortress which occupies the inmost recesses of our soul, a revolution has taken place. Evil passions have reared their heads, and gained the upper hand over the instincts of faith. The struggle is over, and the sentence of banishment has been passed.

Whereas at the moment of baptism the priest has pronounced the words: *Depart, unclean spirit,* it is now the sinner who reverses the formula by which he has been made a Christian, and says:

* Note, too, that Satan can make us the most extravagant offers, for he has not the slightest intention of keeping his promises. Is it not true that invariably, at the moment of temptation, he holds up before our eyes the most radiant pictures of earthly bliss ? "Consent to fall, and you will see what pleasures I promise you !" Whereas, as a matter of fact, what invariably happens is this: We fall into sin, and we find out that this universe—*haec omnia*—this paradise of bliss is of little worth. Once we have fallen into temptation this object which tempted us has no longer the same value in our eyes.

Depart, Holy Spirit. Away—make room—for whom? For the *unclean spirit*. Henceforth I desire that the *unclean spirit* should abide with me. Yes, that is the strange substitute I have chosen for God himself!

Cases of persons outwardly "possessed" by the devil are rare in our times, in civilized countries; but missionaries in far-off lands occasionally report them. For various reasons, God seldom permits any exterior demonstration of the fact that the devil is present within us. This fact, however, makes very little difference.

He who commits a mortal sin is, in the strictest sense of the word, *possessed* by the devil. We do not say possessed *of* the devil, for this expression is consecrated in a very special sense. We say—and it is a fact which can never be too greatly insisted upon—that such a one is possessed *by* the devil.*

At the time of the painful scenes of the Inventories—the "great pity of the churches of France"

---

* Note the difference. Satan enters into the sinner, not *by his substance* (for that is the prerogative of God alone), but *by his operation*—that is to say, by his evil suggestions. Such is the teaching of St Thomas, in commentating the *introivit in eum Satanas* of the gospel (Joan. xii 27, in connection with Judas) and *Contra Gentes*, Book IV, ch. xviii. Fr. Froget writes: "It is the exclusive and unalienable privilege of God . . . to be able to penetrate, by his substance, the inmost recesses of our being. As for the devil, he can, it is true, penetrate in our bodies, move our limbs in spite of the resistance of the will, act on the senses and the imagination, and indirectly on the will, as in the case of demoniacs; but he is powerless to invade the inmost recesses of our being, and to penetrate, at least directly, the sanctuary of the intelligence and the will. If, therefore, he enters into the heart of a man, it is not by his substance, but by the effect of his malice, by the evil thoughts he inspires, and the criminal acts which he suggests, and which he is only too successful in causing to be accomplished" (*De l'Habitation du S. Esprit dans les Ames justes*, p. 59).

—the unscrupulous individuals who caused God to be exiled from certain of our churches, by breaking down the door with hatchets and expelling the faithful who were congregated within, were guilty of profanation.

During the war—which was also the time of " great pity " for these same churches of France— the enemy who bombarded and set fire to the cathedrals, blowing up village spires, and forcing God to take refuge elsewhere—wherever he could— were likewise guilty of profanation. But how infinitely more tragic is the profanation when man banishes God, not from an inanimate temple of stone, but from the living temple of his soul !

The Holy Spirit is no less holy than the sacred Body of our Lord. Of the two kinds of real presence, that of the Third Person within our souls is no less " real " than the presence of the Second Person in the tabernacle.

The ease with which we pillage, and allow to be pillaged, the tabernacle of our hearts can only be accounted for by the fact that we are forgetful of that truth which St Paul insists on, when he exhorts the first Christians to be pure, chaste, and holy; to hate sin so intensely that it would seem an impossibility that they could fall into temptation. " God," he tells them, " dwells within us. We are temples of God."*

* This idea that the human soul is a temple was so familiar to the early Christians that in the epistle attributed to St Barnabas, we find the author consoling them in these terms for the destruction of the Temple at Jerusalem: " The temple has been destroyed. It is no more. Let us see if there be not another temple of God. Before we had embraced the faith, our heart truly resembled the temples raised by men's hands, which were abodes of corruption and weakness. Given up to the worship of idols, it was the abode of demons. All that was in it was God's enemy. But, behold! the Lord will build a temple worthy of his magnificence. By the remission of sins we have

We have now to consider, no longer how the comprehension of the divine Indwelling, by helping us to avoid sin, permits us to draw nearer to God, but how the thought of God within us favours, in the highest degree, the development of this intimacy.

We shall show this by insisting on the different character which this familiarity with the divine Guest in our souls may assume, according as our minds dwell on this or that aspect of the divine presence, this or that Person of the Trinity which dwells, by grace, within us.

---

become new men, an absolutely new creation. So that God truly dwells within us, in the temple of our heart. . . . That is the spiritual temple which the Lord has wrought " (Epistle of St Barnabas, ch. xvi).

BOOK IV

GRACE, AND OUR POSSIBLE RELATIONS WITH GOD WITHIN US

FROM what little we have already said, the reader will have begun to suspect that we can, and indeed *ought* to have the liveliest desire to embrace every opportunity to commune in the most intimate manner possible with the divine Master who dwells, by grace, within our souls. The author of the *Imitation*, indeed, is not afraid to say that we ought to court an *excessive* familiarity, worthy of the excessive familiarity of God—*familiaritas stupenda nimis*.

We will leave on one side, as we said before, any mention of cases of mystical union. We are dealing here with the normal relations—or rather, those which *should be* normal—between every Christian soul and the divine Guest who dwells within it. Moreover, in order that there may be no misunderstanding, we will state exactly what is intended by the word *mystic*.

It means, for our present purpose, either that our faculties, miraculously increased, are rendered capable of perceiving the divine Indwelling in an exceptional manner (and in this sense the presence of God within us, as recognized by faith, will be normal, while the same presence attained by direct experience, which will be, in each case, more or less lively, more or less lasting, and more or less elevated, will be mystical), or else that God, already within us by grace, in the manner we have already described, is manifested as being present in another manner, as, for example, in his Humanity.

Consequently, every phenomenon which has the effect of intensifying to an exceptional degree the normal presence, or of modifying it, or of adding to it another, may be called mystical.

While leaving such cases out of the question, we would at the same time remark that if, in theory, the line of division may readily be drawn between normal piety and extraordinary states of soul, in practice the mystical life, at any rate in its beginnings, is nothing more than the flowering of the life of grace which is common to all souls who are not in a state of mortal sin. In other words, Christians do not become mystics because they possess something *different* from us, but because they possess *better*, and in a more eminent manner, the divine Guest.

The life of God within us is the foundation, not only of a life of normal piety, but also of the mystical life. " Let us suppose," says Fr. L. de Grandmaison, " that a Christian who is in a state of grace succeeds, by natural means, in developing a sort of intellectual intuition of his soul. He will enjoy a vision which substantially resembles that which marks the dawn of the mystic state, but without perceiving to be such the sweetness and the supernatural benefits he enjoys."

This general consideration having been laid down, we will now proceed to find out what ought to be the normal relations between the Christian and

(1) God the Father;
(2) God the Son; and
(3) God the Holy Ghost.

CHAPTER I

WITH GOD THE FATHER

" You must understand that you are not the man
God wishes you to be, the-true man, as God con-
ceived him, and as you yourself conceive him to be
when, in your lucid moments, your ideal *you* hovers
within sight. What have you made of your life
so far ? Where are your titles to divine adoption ?
Are you indeed a child of God, in works, and in
thought ? No. Then weep for the life you have
profaned, and rendered vain and sterile, and in the
first tear you shed you will find God."

These are the words of Fr. Gratry to the man
who is leading a sinful life.

But do those souls who remain habitually or
constantly in a state of grace realize what resources
are given them by this divine adoption by the
Father who is in heaven—an adoption which
endows them with the very life of the Father,
present within their souls, in so far as a creature
may participate in it, and in proportion as that
creature, by his virtuous life, opens the door of his
heart that God may enter in ?

Human adoption is a legal matter. It endows
the adopted person with the name, the armorial
bearings, and the inheritance of his adopted father,
but it cannot infuse that father's blood into his
veins.

Divine adoption, however, enables us actually
to partake of the nature of God. We have St
Peter's solemn assurance on this point : *ut per
haec efficiamini divinae consortes naturae*—that by

these you may be made partakers of the divine nature.*

"We cannot doubt," says the author of *Vers les Cimes*,† "that the higher life promised and granted to us by Jesus Christ is the participation in the life of God himself. Its origin is made clear to us. It is derived from the bosom of the Father, like the Word himself. It has been prepared and elaborated for us by the Son who bought it for us by his sacrifice. This source which has been put within men's reach is distributed, at his pleasure, by the Holy Ghost, who causes it to flow within our souls by mysterious forces. Thus, all those who have received it have become sons of God, born, in this higher sense, not of the blood, nor of the desire, nor of the will of man, but of God. We are truly participators in the divine nature. A divine seed is implanted in us. We bear God in our bodies. We are animated and guided by the spirit of God. The divine transforms us, as fire transforms iron, and, filled with the divinity, we are the temples of the living God."

There can be no better summing up of our supernatural existence, and of the nature of the relations which we can, and ought to, have with the divine Trinity, and with God the Father in particular.

In a word, we have become, not metaphorically, but really, *filii Dei*—sons of God.

It follows, then, for those of us who have grasped something of what the doctrine of sanctifying grace means, that the soul which enjoys the privilege of being numbered among the sons of God owes the Father *filial affection*.

* 2 Peter i 4. See, too, the Offertory of the Mass: *divinitatis consortes*—participators in the divinity.

† *Exhortations à un jeune Homme chrétien*, by the Abbé Chabot. Beauchesne, 1909, p. 242.

What a difference between the sovereign lord who is content to deal with his creatures merely as his *things*, and the loving Father; between the far-away God who takes advantage of his remoteness to make us feel the great difference between us and him, and the God who is so near at hand and so willing to overlook the difference between us and him that he actually takes up his abode with us!

Once man was a subject, a slave. Now he is a member of the family. He can call God not only " the Father," but *his* Father. He is the brother of Jesus, and together they say *our Father*. He is of the same blood as Jesus, and Jesus is of the same blood as his Father. Jesus is The Son, but man may likewise call himself *son*, by adoption, it is true, for Jesus shares the divine substance by nature, whereas man shares it by grace. Nevertheless, he has a perfect right to the title of son, and, moreover, he has been chosen among a thousand, for " of his own will hath he begotten us by the word of truth."*

Likewise, because we are sons of God, we have " received the spirit of adoption of sons, whereby we cry: Abba (Father),"† and it likewise follows that we have the right of inheritance.

Our Elder Brother has no wish to seize everything for himself. No, indeed. His sole purpose in coming down to earth was to enable us to gain possession of it, that we might share in his happiness.

His sojourn here below accomplished, did he not return to the Father to prepare a place for us? And one day he will return to fetch us, for he is determined that where he is, there also shall we be.

Then it will no longer be a question of an obscure

* Epistle of St James, i 18.
† Rom. viii 15.

communion in the miniature heaven of our souls—
that divine " home " in which he is pleased to
dwell. It will be a communion face to face, in
broad daylight, and the boundless joy of a boundless heaven. *Intra in gaudium domini tui.**

What is death? asked a certain pious soul. It
is a leap on to the Father's knees. Our present
position is only provisionary, and those who have
given heed to this fact feel a sense of exile.
*Expectatio creaturae revelationem filiorum Dei ex-
pectat . . . quia et ipsa creatura liberatur a servitute
corruptionis in libertatem gloriae filiorum Dei.
Scimus enim quod omnis creatura ingemiscit et
parturit usque adhuc.* The expectation of the
creature waiteth for the revelation of the sons of
God. . . . Because the creature also itself shall
be delivered from the servitude of corruption, into
the liberty of the glory of the sons of God. For we
know that every creature groaneth and *travaileth
in pain, even until now.*†

It hath not yet appeared what we shall be.‡

One day, this provisionary state will cease to be,
and, entering into the possession of our heritage,
we shall see expanding before our eyes " the glorious
liberty of the children of God."

The hour will strike when all that is doomed to
perish within us will be absorbed by life—*ut ab-
sorbeatur quod mortale est a vita.* All this God has
thus prepared for our glorification, in pledge whereof
he has given us the Spirit, the source of our higher
life. *Qui autem efficit nos in hoc ipsum, Deus qui
dedit nobis pignus Spiritus.*§

Then we shall be *made perfect in one.*

Christ came for no other reason than that we
might partake, even in this life, of the life of the
Father, which is also his life, and that this life

---

* Matt. xxv 21.   † Rom. viii 19-22.
‡ 1 John iii 2.   § 2 Cor. v 4 and 5.

might dwell and expand in us eternally. For this he prayed to the Father: " That they all may be one, as thou, Father, in me, and I in thee; that they also may be one in us, I in them, and thou in me, that they may be made perfect in one."*

Is there, in truth, any other history which has the same power to captivate our hearts—any history, save the history of the life of God in our souls, hidden, as far as this world is concerned, but in heaven splendid and radiant ?

Is there any geography that will bear comparison with that of the myriad streams of grace which flow silently throughout the world; which expand into deep, and in most cases invisible, lakes; and which, in spite of every obstacle, push their way through sand, and wreckage, and poisonous filth to the boundless ocean ?

Is there any drama which can compare with that of the soul in which God himself is pleased to dwell, but which will have none of him; or of that other soul in which God no longer dwells, and which lies in loving wait for his return, until at last he, who has sought it for so long, is once more united to it, by tears of repentance, so that the gates of love are once more thrown open, and the dead city stirs to new life ?

Alas! how few Christians think on these things ! How few have that filial affection for the Father of the family which the fact of our divine adoption permits, and demands of us to cherish ! Yet how easy it would be to experience this devotion, if we did but rightly understand the meaning of the prayer our Lord himself has taught us—the *Our Father*.

I say purposely *the* prayer.

When our Lord teaches his apostles this prayer he does not say: This is *one* prayer among others

* John xvii 21-23.

which you may use. This is an example, a model, of the prayers you may say.

No. He says: *Thus therefore shall you pray.** Thus, and not otherwise.

We have not, then, several examples or specimens of Christian prayer. *The* Christian prayer is the prayer of Christ, the *Pater*, composed by Christ for the use of Christians. *Thus shall you pray.* The tone is categorical and imperative.

The *Pater*, then, is not only the first of all prayers. It is the only prayer.

This does not mean that it is an invariable formula; a prayer which precludes all spontaneous outburst, all personal and natural raising of the individual soul. It means that it is a prayer of which every other prayer, if it is to be *Christian*, should be not a reproduction, an expansion, or, better still, a development; a prayer which will suffer no substantial modification, and will admit of no capital addition; a prayer which is the type of all prayers, the fundamental prayer, and, consequently, that to which all others should be traced back; on which all others should be modelled; by which all others should be checked; and which all others should faithfully reflect. When you pray, thus shall you pray. You shall say: *Our Father....*

For the *Pater* is none other than the backbone of all private prayer; the essence of our personal piety, and of our interior life, as well as of all liturgical prayer; and the theme which inspires and quickens each and every step in our path to the stars.

Our Father....

Many people see in these touching words nothing but a flattering form of address, calculated to attract the good graces of him "who reigns in heaven."

* Matt. vi 9.

They mean very much more than that. They express a fact of the utmost importance, and one round which our whole spiritual life should revolve, and from which all Christian activity should radiate.

Once we were children of wrath—*filii irae*. The *Pater* reminds us that we are now children of God. We are so used to this expression that it no longer strikes us. We are *children of God*. We find nothing extraordinary in that. We feel it is almost our right. Nevertheless, to be able to call God our *Father* when we were as nothing; to be able to call him our Father, when we are but sinful creatures—surely this is enough to make us pause and think.

But no! It does not surprise us in the very least! Yet St Paul marvelled at the thought of it. I may cry to God, Abba, Father! I, call God my Father? It can never be! By myself it would be impossible. But I possess within me the Spirit, the Holy Ghost, the Spirit of the Father, and it is this Spirit which recognizes in God the Fatherhood which I acclaim.

What a consolation this knowledge that the Father regards us with a father's, and even with a mother's eye, ought to be to us in our lives!

Our Lord took pains to bring this truth home to us. A mother, he says, loves much, but the Heavenly Father loves you a hundredfold more. See the lilies of the field, how they are clothed. Solomon in all his glory did not equal them in splendour. Behold, in this their beauty, the Father's gift. See the birds of the air. Will he who created them leave them without food or shelter? Behold, in this care of them, the Father's love. And if God has such care for the lilies and the birds, how much more will his care be for you!

Our Father—two words which proclaim the most beautiful of all God's titles; that which should be placed before all others, as a preface, a reminder, and a check.

He is just—yes, but he is a Father. He is terrible, yes, when necessary—but always, even then, he is a Father.

How sad it is, then, to find so many Christians— even good Christians—failing to recognize this, and consequently giving way on every occasion to want of trust in him. A trial overtakes them. They accuse God. They treat him almost as a savage. God, a savage? Have these Christians ever meditated on the first two words of the *Our Father?*

We have fallen into sin, and not by any means for the first time. We give way to feelings of discouragement. We had made such good resolutions, and now we have fallen again! God will never pardon us.

God will bear malice? Can an earthly father bear malice? No. And can we imagine for a moment that our Heavenly Father, he who made the hearts of those earthly fathers, bears malice either? What foolishness! If we have sinned, let us at least not add to our sin another, and a thousand times more grave than all our other sins put together—that of doubting our Father's love. That, more than all else, would prove that we were not his sons.

Does the Prodigal Son think, for a single moment, that his father will reject him? No, indeed. " I will arise," he says, " and go in haste to find my kind father." *Surgam . . . ad Patrem!*

A truly filial spirit includes, in the first place, a desire for the glory and honour of him whose children we are; and if we turn to the Our Father we shall see that this desire is expressed in three forms.

Hallowed be thy Name ! How painful are all the blasphemies of individuals and of governments, and how deeply we should desire to compensate our Father for such insults by as many more acts of love !

Thy Kingdom come ! As soon as we begin really to consider God as a Father, how ardently we shall long that his fatherly hand may be extended to every individual, every family, and every nation !

Thy Will be done ! What a consolation, what a feeling of relief the knowledge that *God is our Father* brings with it ! So many misfortunes are apt to overtake us. What is God doing ? He is doing *his will*. But he is acting like an executioner ! No—like a Father. A Father ? It does not look like it ! But when I begin to look a little closer I see better, and I begin to realize that come what may, for good or for evil, one thing is certain—that the Father means me, personally, to turn it into a means of sanctification—*haec est voluntas Dei, sanctificatio vestra*—and that he sees things which are hidden from me, and that our Lord himself has given me an example, in the *Agony in the Garden*, when he uttered his *fiat voluntas tua*, of the meaning of real filial devotion to the Father. Yes, Father, I desire what you desire, because you desire it, as you desire it, and as much as you desire it.

As well as being the charter of the rights of God, the *Pater* is the charter of our rights as Christians.

We are sons, and everything follows from that fact. As sons we can go to the Father and ask— for we have his authority to do so—for everything to which sons have a right.

So far, in the *Pater*, we have been expressing wishes, and repeating divine commands. Our Father has said: Hallowed be my Name, and we, his sons, have taken up the words: Yes, Father! Hallowed be thy Name !—and so on.

But now man is asking for favours on his own behalf. He is claiming his rights, as the Father's son.

He is a son—and he has the right to be fed.

Father, give us bread !

He is a son—and he has a right to claim the Father's indulgence.

Father, forgive us our sins !

He is a son—and he has a right to the Father's protection.

Father, deliver us from evil !

That is what prayer means. It means " living at home "—not only with our own soul, but with the Divine Family which dwells there with us. It means living gladly in the bosom of this Family, without care for the morrow, with the certainty of being understood and of having our petitions granted, or, better still, forestalled, and of being enveloped in loving solicitude.

Moreover, let no one object that this is just a matter of " sentiment." Quite the contrary. It is a matter of faith, and is founded directly on the teaching of the Church.

There was founded, one year, at Villepinte, an " association of gratitude " consecrated to the blessed Virgin. The formula adopted by one of the children ran as follows: " Mother, I know that you are good; that you love me; and that you are powerful. That is enough for me."

Why should we not address such words as these to God ? " Father, I know that you are good; that you love me; and that you are powerful. That is enough for me."

This is the true filial spirit. Is it the spirit which always animates our souls ? Is anything lacking to inspire us with such feelings as these ?

CHAPTER II

WITH THE WORD

THE Word came down from heaven that he might give us life—life abounding—his own life, the life of God, forfeited by Adam.

For no other reason did he come.   Only for this. Let us consider for a moment the magnificence of his divine life within us, and the grandeur of our souls, which have been " naturalized divine."

" In the beginning was the Word "—the Second Person of the Adorable Trinity—" and the Word was with God, and the Word was God."*

In the Word was life, that life which God had willed from the beginning that man should share, and which, by a mark of love, he desires to restore to us, in spite of our sin.

The Word becomes flesh.   The life that was once far from our grasp is brought near.   Of an essence too pure to be received by us, it will be compressed into a humanity like unto our own, together to form the Humanity of Christ.   The life of the Word becomes the life of the Man-God.

From this Man-God life will flow to other men, all called to become " conformable to his image "† who is the true Son of the Father.   And, behold, by grace we become the brothers of Jesus Christ, " the first-born of many brethren."‡

This idea—that we are the brethren of Jesus, who is the Elder Brother—makes a great impression on some souls.   Those who followed—or dare read, even—a certain *triduum* by Père Longhaye,

* John i 1.   † Rom. viii 29.   ‡ *Ibid.*

which was devoted entirely to this theme, will have realized what treasures repay the efforts of anyone who takes the trouble to meditate on this point.

Some feel a certain repugnance at the idea that Christ should be called our Elder Brother. It seems to them to lack respect.

Such souls are in the habit of picturing God as a terrible Jehovah, surrounded by thunder and lightning, whom we must approach with bare feet, and ashes on our heads. God's justice, his majesty —these are the themes which inspire their piety. Whether it is from a habit of meditating on their weakness and their falls, or a natural tendency, or a preference for reading the Old Testament, or a training tainted with Jansenism, or the memory of terrible stories related in some long-ago Retreat, or read in some book—at all events they are largely governed by the idea of this aspect of God's greatness.

Others—as, for example, the author of the *Imitation*, at least as far as the last two books are concerned—though no less respectful of God's majesty, are struck, above all, by the efforts he makes to hide his power and to draw close to us. They do not, indeed, disdain the Law-giver, but they prefer to think of God, above all, as the Friend.

For such souls, just as there can be no intimacy without presence, so there can be none without a certain equality; and since this equality does, indeed, exist, they make it the central idea round which their whole life revolves.

Turn, for example, to the magnificent thirteenth chapter of the fourth book of the *Imitation* : *Quis mihi det, Domine, ut inveniam te solum et aperiam tibi totum cor meum. . . . Tu in me, et ego in te,*

et sic nos in unum pariter manere concede—" Who
will give me, Lord, to find you, and you alone,
and to offer you my whole heart. . . .   You in
me, I in you, and therefore, together, evermore
to dwell."

A similar aspect of this idea—or rather, the same
aspect but seen from a particular angle—is the
dogma of the Communion of Saints.
The study of Jesus, the Elder Brother, soon
teaches us to take an interest in our other brothers,
who are also his.
As soon as these our brothers are not rooted in
Christ, divine life is not within them, and we feel
impelled, therefore, to seek them out, and to tell
them what they have to do in order that death
may no longer have dominion over them. *Non
de vestra tantum salute, sed de universo mundo.* The
lamp of zeal is lit by the sight of so many dead
bodies, instead of so many living souls: *Nonne
vivent ossa ista?* The world seems to resemble
the plain of Ezechiel's vision, for the souls in which
the life of Christ does not circulate can be said to
be like nothing better than dry bones.
To what purpose, then, did the Elder Brother
come down from heaven, to die upon the Cross, if,
after all these centuries, the world is still the abode
of so many unfaithful souls? This is a thought
which makes us feel literally responsible for the
salvation of the world.
We seem to be on the borders of a vast
desert, and from over the dry expanse of sand
there comes to us a passionate lament. " What
is that noise?" asks the traveller to the Sahara.
" It is the cry of the desert. It bewails its fate,
for it would fain be a prairie," answers his Arab
guide.
And some irresistible impulse prompts you to

arise, and to go forth to tell abroad the story of
the Samaritan woman; of the mysterious water
which gushed forth unto eternal life; the living
and life-giving water which can quench every
thirst. You feel you must set out, carrying with
you as much of this water as you are able, to give
drink to parched souls—to as many souls as possible
—even to every single soul.

A young airman once had a terrible fall from his
'plane while fighting against two adversaries. He
remained for twenty-four hours inside the lines.
Already the desire to give himself to God had taken
root in his heart. He was picked up on the first
Friday of the month with a broken spine. Henceforth his mind was made up. " I am still on my
poor back, and unable to move," he writes, " but
the paralysis is slowly disappearing. I am going
to be completely cured. I must be cured, for God
wills it, for he has filled my soul with *immense
ambition and gigantic dreams.*"*

Or it may be that what strikes us is not so much
the idea of those souls in distant lands to whom
the gospel has not been preached, as that of the
souls around us who once shared the life of the
Elder Brother, and now have lost or squandered
it, so that they, too, have become like so many
corpses in the land of the living.

That man whom I see passing . . . is he to be
numbered among the living, or the dead ? What
can I do for him ? Shall I be Cain to his Abel ?
Have I been in any way responsible for his loss ?
If I can honestly say that I am not responsible,
have I yet no duty towards him ?

Does he not need my help, that he may be restored

* See our *Immolations fécondes* (Bloud et Gay),
pp. 3-11.

to life, and am I going to make the old excuse:
" Am I my brother's keeper ?"

There are few of us who are not in some way
responsible for the souls of others. How many of
us realize our duty in this respect ? All these
people whom I employ, who surround me, who
obey my orders, who live with me, who help me,
or serve me—are they all *alive ?*

Ponder over this examination of conscience:

" You confide a formidable and a divine mission,
Lord Jesus, to every man who has charge of the
soul of a child. By example, by word, with discretion, and the profound respect due to his intelligence, and his free-will, the educator must strive
to bring you to birth in the child's soul. Every
educator is a prophet, who announces and makes
ready for Christmas in the soul of the child.
For the young men whose names I now remember before you—have my words, my actions, and
my silences too made ready and accomplished
your birth in their hearts? Lord Jesus, I pray
for them, that you may come and take possession of their souls. Lord, make them true
Christians."*

Thus the mysterious, but very real, tie which
binds our souls to Jesus Christ and to eternal
life brings us naturally to consider the tie—also
mysterious, but very real—which unites us with
all Christian souls.

Ut sint . . . unum.†

All these lives must be one. All " connected
up " with Christ, they are subject to that law of
communicating vessels to which we have already
alluded.

* *Bulletin des Professeurs catholiques de l'Université*
(Pierre Pacary, Christmas, 1921).

† *Ego in eis, et tu in me, ut sint consummati in unum.*
There is perfect unity between God, Christ, and ourselves.
We are " made perfect in unity " (John xvii 23).

If life diminishes, or ceases to flow, within any one soul, the whole is deprived—slightly, or to a great extent—of life. If, on the contrary, it increases, then the whole will benefit in proportion.

Ut sint unum. Read the sermon of St Augustine which is found in the breviary of the Feast of the Dedication of a Church. All Christians, he says, together form the Mystical Body of Christ. Jesus is the living corner-stone, and we are the other living stones of this temple. Jesus, and those of us Christians who are in a state of grace, all form a single block, a single *whole*, a single cathedral, a single heart, a single love, and a single entity—the only something, the only all.

Thus may souls live in union with one another, and with God may heart beat with heart, lending each other strength and virtue, and sanctifying one another, each member deriving strength from the others.

" The prompting of grace which brings about my salvation may be directly due to an act of love accomplished either this morning or five hundred years ago, by a totally unknown individual, who now receives his reward. See that poor girl praying in a poor devastated church. All she knows is that God will certainly hear her, because he has promised to grant the petitions of all who ask with confidence. Listen, and you will hear the sound of foot-soldiers, and horsemen, and chariots break the silence of the night—and this sound is the movements of the lips of this innocent child to whose petition God must infallibly give ear."

What encouragement to our spiritual life will lie in this thought—that the smallest act of virtue we accomplish, by increasing within our souls the flow of divine life, increases it likewise in all those who are in a state of grace, and to whom we are united in Christ.

Other souls make another use of the great idea of the Mystical Body.

The Word came down, and was made flesh, in order to be a *mediator ;* and it is his wish that all who will consent to share his mission should be associated with him in his work of redemption. It is his desire that our co-operation should be necessary, not because he cannot of himself accomplish the task, but because his love prompts him to ask our help.

He is the *First*, but he wants us to be his " seconds." Alone he could have saved all souls, yet some souls will only be saved with our help.

In this resides the peculiar dignity—and the awful responsibility—of the Christian soul.

It is this consideration that has prompted certain souls to share, in as far as they are able, in the experience of the Word, in the sacred Humanity of Christ, and to offer themselves to be, as Sister Elizabeth of the Holy Trinity puts it so happily, " a surplus humanity."

What possibilities of suffering such an obligation involves, only those elect souls themselves dare to contemplate.

To supplement the work of Christ, to share in his mission—they know very well what that involves. It involves a share in his Passion. And behold, we see how, in their case, the real understanding of what is meant by a state of grace leads not only, as in those other cases we have mentioned, to a *spirit of fraternity*, but even to a *spirit of total sacrifice*.

" Host with host, host for host, that, it seems to me, ought to be a summary of my life."*

Whence comes this strange ambition on the part

* *Une Ame réparatrice.* Simone Denniel (Vitte, 1916).

of certain souls to offer themselves as victims ?
We have tried elsewhere to indicate the answer.*

The sight of Christ hanging on the Cross; the
longing to put an offering in the alms-box of his
gaping wounds; the thought that they can offer
the Master the shelter of their hearts, and there,
by sheer love, generosity, and devotion, make him
forget all the abominations committed by the
wicked; the knowledge of the unheard-of possibility
that their sacrifice may make reparation for all
those who forget, and all those who outrage him;
and that their humanity may be an instrument for
suffering with, instead of, and on behalf of Jesus
himself—all this is more than enough to inflame
their zeal.

They accept, moreover, all that the boldest of
spiritual writers have said concerning the *spirit of
death* as if it were the most natural, the most binding,
and the most obvious thing in the world.

For these souls the *quotidie morior* of the Apostle
is no mere formula, no phrase to pass over lightly,
leaving it to others to take it to heart. There is
no need for St Paul to implore of such souls to
*put off according to former conversation the old
man, who is corrupted according to the desire of
error. And put on the new man, who according to
God is created in justice, and holiness, and truth.*†
They are eager to say, with him: *With Christ I
am nailed to the Cross,*‡ and *I glory in the cross of
our Lord Jesus.*§

In the celebrated play, *L'Aiglon*, the Austrian
minister, Metternicht, in order to discourage the

* Article in the *Messager du S. Cœur*, published as a
pamphlet: *Ames réparatrices* (Apostolat de la Prière,
Toulouse). See also: *Pourquoi l'on part* (*Revue de la
Jeunesse*, July 10, 1914; and, above all, *The Ideal of
Reparation* (London, 1920).

† Eph. iv 22 and 24.
‡ Gal. ii 19. § Gal. iv 16.

hero of the piece, tells him that he has inherited
none of those qualities of his father which went to
make him a good sovereign.

" You have the little hat—but not the head for it !"

It is not, however, to discourage us, but rather
to spur us on to greater efforts, that our consciences
are constantly whispering similar words to us:
Gaze on the countenance of your suffering Lord.
Do you resemble him ? Compare your countenance. Is it that of one crucified ?

The sight of the mangled body of our Lord makes
us lose the courage to live without the Cross, and
to determine to be, at whatever cost, among those
whom God " foreknew, and predestined to be made
conformable to the image of his Son."

More than that—all those souls who live an
interior life are destined to find themselves—sometimes more, sometimes less, but *always*—marked out
for suffering.

It is not that they will be called upon to suffer
the physical agony of St Lydwine of Schiedam, for
instance, but that interiorly, and constantly, they
will be crucified. They feel that there is such a
gulf between what they are and what they fain
would be. They feel that the divine Guest demands
their *whole hearts*, and they realize what a sacrifice
that involves. They long to be his, alone and
entirely, and yet they withhold from him their best.

And then, even if in their most generous moments
they feel they are giving their all, how insignificant
does the offering appear ! They feel it is no better
than *nothing*. They cannot compete with him.
He is too rich. They are too poor. The odds are
against them, and they always lose the game. It
is Jacob wrestling with the angel. The angel
always wins.

So much for *themselves*. But what about those *around* them? Christ is so little known, so badly served. The tide of sin mounts higher and higher, and threatens to submerge the whole land, while the space which it leaves uncovered is nothing but a plain, or so many islands of indifference.

What is to be done? The desire to help is not lacking. It is the means that are so inadequate. See the agony of Francis Xavier's last moments, when his eyes linger for the last time on the vast expanses of China which he will never traverse; the agony of the missionary who has toiled for fifty years, and who, from the station where, wayworn, he lies drawing his last breath, is forced to watch the building of a gigantic pagoda dedicated, not to the Christ whom he has served, but to some greasy and contemptible Buddha; the agony of St Francis of Assisi, as he paces the lonely paths of La Verna, from which he can gaze on that Umbrian countryside which was his world, and murmurs: "Jesus is not loved! Jesus is not loved!"

"Why can I not encourage everyone to love Jesus Christ my master, and persuade all men to enter his service?" writes M. Olier.

"Blessed be God, who supplements with such sweetness and charity the zeal of his poor servants who fret themselves to death because they can only serve him, who is such a great master, for such a short time, and so imperfectly. Thousands and thousands of millions of men filled with love of you and zeal to do your service, to come to give my joy what is lacking to it; a hundred thousand, and as many years again, during which I could spread a holy ambition to procure your glory, and that of your Son, and his holy Mother—that is what is wanted in order at least to begin to accomplish the desire that burns within me.

" Oh, if I had as many hearts as there are of damned and unhappy spirits who blaspheme you, how willingly would I employ them to sing your praises, and make up to you the honours which they refuse you ! How gladly would I multiply my tongue into as many creatures as you have placed on the earth, to glorify your name !

" But, O my God, in order to make up for it, let me lose myself in your Jesus, in him who is your eternal praise, and who renders you infinitely infinite honours. Let me plunge myself, and bury myself in the hearts of your saints. Let me, like David, invite every living creature to sing your praises. Let me, as far as in me lies, unite the whole world to your glory.

" It is for my Jesus, and for his members. It is for him and for me that all in the whole universe has been made, and all has been destined to be, in Jesus Christ your Son, and in his members a victim of praise, to the glory of thy name, for all eternity. O God, my love, let me begin now, never to leave off."*

Piety takes many different forms. Some souls love best to think of our Lord as the Word, while others prefer to dwell on his sacred Humanity.

You will remember the prayer of St Ignatius: " O beloved Word of God, teach me to be generous, to serve you as you deserve to be served, to give without counting the cost, to fight without fear of being wounded, to work without seeking rest, and to spend myself without expecting any other reward than the knowledge that I am doing your holy will."

Sister Elizabeth of the Trinity also had a special devotion to the " Beloved Word of God," but under

* See the *Life of M. Olier*, published by Lebel, 1818, Versailles, pp. 603-632.

a particular aspect which is precisely that which we are considering in the present work—that of the Word present within the justified soul. Her beautiful prayer loses nothing by comparison with that of St Ignatius:

" O Eternal Word, Word of my God, I desire to spend my whole life in listening to you. I desire to make myself teachable of all, that I may learn all from you. Then, through all the darkness, all the emptiness, all the impotence, I desire always to gaze on you, and to remain under your great light.

" O, *Consuming Fire*, spirit of love, come upon me, in order that there may be, as it were, an incarnation of the Word within my soul. Let me be a surplus humanity, in which he renews all his Mystery. And do you, O Father, bend down to your little creature, and see in her the beloved in whom you have placed all your love. . . ."

Certain souls love, above all else, to meditate upon the Holy Infancy.

Everyone has read the life of another Carmelite nun, Blessed Teresa of the Child Jesus, and those who consider it to be lacking in virility are making a very great mistake. It means more than appears at first sight to offer oneself to our Lord to be like a ball in the hands of a little child, to be thrown down, pricked with a nail or a pin, played with, or left neglected in a corner. The great St Teresa herself had a special devotion to the Holy Child, after the celebrated vision on the staircase: " Who art thou ?" " I, Lord, am Teresa of Jesus." " And I am Jesus of Teresa."

While he was yet young St Antony is said to have had a similar vision. One day he saw before him a little child with his apron turned up, and appearing to be looking for some treasure. " What dost thou want ?" " I want thy heart." ' What dost thou do ?" " Thou dost see. I am on earth,

7

seeking for the hearts that will consent to give me their love."

During the last visit which M. Olier paid him, Père de Condren, being about to die, gave him one last piece of advice: " Take the Child Jesus for your director "—" words," adds M. Olier, " which have proved very useful and very precious to me."

The Spirit of Childhood is a spirit which is habitual among those who lead an interior life, for whom the contemplation of the childhood of our Lord remains no mere object of sterile meditation, but ends in being a swift and spontaneous habit of faith, and to the complete submission necessary in order that God may abide in us, according to his desire, and as much as he desires.

" All the morning our Lord entertained me with this thought, that what I most needed was to obtain the spirit of the holy childhood . . . to be a child who can neither speak nor walk, nor help himself; who is turned this way or that at will, without his being consulted, or told the reason why. And I let this thought sink into me, when I listened to Jesus, my Teacher: Amen, I say unto you, unless you be born again, you shall not see the kingdom of God. You must be born again. . . . Suffer the children to come unto me, for the kingdom is theirs, and of those who resemble them. I gazed on Jesus our Model, the Jesus of the Incarnation, of the crib, of the flight into Egypt, of Nazareth. What silence, what dependence, what abandonment !"*

Only those Christians who have acquired this childlike simplicity, by meditating on our Lord's Infancy, know how far this " second birth "—the birth of God in our hearts by grace, which makes us " children of the kingdom "—may lead them, and what sacrifices it may involve.

* Pauline Reynolds, a convert and a Carmelite nun.

To an even greater extent does an understanding of the mystery of the Indwelling develop the *eucharistic spirit* among us.

It may seem at first sight that our devotion to God present within our souls will tend to diminish our devotion to God present in the tabernacles of our churches. From the moment I possess the *spiritual presence* the *eucharistic presence* is less necessary, less desirable, and I can more easily dispense with receiving God in Holy Communion from the mere fact that he is already present within me.

This is a superficial, and therefore mistaken point of view. The more often souls commune with the God who dwells within them, the greater will be their desire to become *eucharistic souls*. I use this expression, not only because the more they realize the divine treasure they possess, the more they will live in *thanksgiving*, which, translated literally, means *eucharist*,* but also because it follows, logically, that such souls will experience an ardent desire to receive our Lord in Holy Communion.

He who loves desires to love more. He who possesses desires to possess still more, and in every possible manner. Undoubtedly, to possess *God* is the chief thing, and this is taken for granted in communion, since it is necessary that in order to receive it, we should be in a state of grace. But when we add to this possession that of the sacred Humanity of the Redeemer, we enjoy a signal privilege, and the more so because, together with the sacred Humanity, we entertain within our souls by Holy Communion more also of his divinity.

Those persons who lead an interior life are well aware of this, and for this reason, far from being

* The post-communion of the Mass for the feast of St Aloysius makes us ask in imitation of the model held up for our edification, that we may live *eucharistically*—dwell in thanksgiving: *in gratiarum actione manere.*

inclined to go less frequently to Holy Communion, they will be eager to approach the altar-rails as frequently as possible.

They know that a single word suffices in order to transubstantiate the altar-bread, but that, in order to transubstantiate us ourselves more than one host is necessary, and that it will be necessary for the Son to come again and again in order to make us as perfect as we are required to be—as perfect (and no less) as the Father himself: *sicut Pater coelestis*.

Moreover, those souls who best realize the mystery of the divine Indwelling will, more than any others, understand the Eucharist in the highest sense. They will realize that if they receive a Victim, they also are called to make an oblation of themselves. By meditating on the *temples of God* which they are, they will readily perceive that their hearts should be the place of a liturgical offering, an intimate sanctuary, wherein they will be called upon to bring as a sacrifice every movement of their souls, according to the invitation of St Paul that we should be like Christ, *a living sacrifice, holy and pleasing to God*,* and that, in this sense, they are endowed, as we read in St Peter and the Apocalypse, with true priesthood.†

If the thought of *God within Us* fosters devotion to the holy Eucharist, it can also be said that this thought, and this alone, provides us with an adequate explanation of true devotion to the *Sacred Heart*.

Fr. Ramière proves this beyond any doubt in his

* Rom. xii 1. See the author's *Ideal of Reparation*. '

† *Fecisti nos . . . sacerdotes*. Thou hast made us priests (Apoc. v 10). See also 1 Pet. ii 5 and 9. We have explained the mystical priesthood of every Christian and the obligations it entails in a *Récollection* published by *Prêtres-Soldats de France* (August 10, 1918: *L'Esprit sacerdotal*).

beautiful book, *Le Cœur de Jésus et la Divinisation du Chrétien*.

The flow of divine life within our souls is undoubtedly the work of all three Persons of the Holy Trinity. The First and Third Persons contribute to it no less than the Second, for this process consists in our adoption by God the Father, and in the union of our souls with the Holy Spirit.

But it is by Jesus Christ that the divine Spirit is given us, and it is solely on account of our incorporation with Jesus Christ that God the Father recognizes and loves us as his children.

Our justification is the work of Jesus. Can we say, asks Fr. Ramière, that it is the work of the *Heart of Jesus?* Yes, he replies: we can—and we ought.

Did our Lord procure our justification of his own free will, or from necessity? He acted *freely*. The Word came down *willingly—quia voluit*. And the sacred Humanity of the Redeemer freely ratified this free act. "God willingly engendered us," says St James. And St Paul says: *Dilexit me, tradidit se*. He saved me out of pure love, moved purely by the impulse of his heart.

If Jesus Christ, continues Fr. Ramière, gives us his Spirit, and makes us his members, it is purely by an act of free will, which is constantly renewed by his love. It is therefore to his heart, the organ (or, better, the symbol) of his love, that we owe our divine life, and all our supernatural riches.*

Thus, by the first and overflowing transport of his love—*propter nimiam caritatem qua dilexit nos*—our Lord wrought our salvation, by shedding the last drop of his blood.

By another and unceasing transport of love, he obtains for us, at every moment of our lives, through his merits, the sanctifying grace of which we have constant need. Hence the saying of St Paul: *He*

* *Divinisation du Chrétien*, p. 565.

is our justice [*i.e.*, it is he who renders us just], our sanctification, and our redemption.*

In heaven our Lord spends his time—or rather his eternity—in sending us the Holy Spirit. It was to one act of love—of his heart—that we owe the first and great day of Pentecost. Each individual Pentecost, each descent of the Holy Spirit in our souls, is also an act of his love—of his heart. "When I say: 'Jesus,'" adds Fr. Ramière, "I see God made accessible. When I say 'Heart of Jesus' I see the Saviour even nearer. I see in his heart the point at which he desires to unite himself to me, and at which he invites me to unite myself to him."

The Heart of Jesus is the power-station of that fountain which gushes forth into life eternal—*fons aquae salientis in vitam aeternam*. By its action the divine influx, the Holy Spirit, reaches every member of the Mystical Body. Every act of our supernatural life is the act of Christ, for to his Person (who is our head) are mystically united ours (who are the members), and it is through his heart that life circulates from the head to the members—from him to us.

In every language the heart is the symbol of love. It is not surprising, then, that Christ, to whose love we owe our salvation, should say to Margaret Mary: "Behold my heart, which has done so much for men."

To separate devotion to the Sacred Heart from the dogma of the divine Indwelling is to run the risk of making it a purely sentimental devotion, without either definite source or obvious aim.

Those souls, on the other hand, who have a right understanding of what is meant by a state of grace and of the divine Indwelling will infallibly practise an ardent devotion to the Sacred Heart of our Lord —to that heart to which they owe the spiritual riches whose possession they enjoy.

* 1 Cor. i 30.

CHAPTER III

WITH THE HOLY SPIRIT

" Have you received the Spirit ?" were the words of St Paul to the Ephesians.*

We know the answer we can give to this question. We remember the words of the priest at our baptism: *Depart, unclean spirit, and give place to the Holy Spirit.* If, then, we have not fallen into mortal sin, or if, having done so, we have received absolution and are in a state of grace, we can reply that we " have received the Spirit."

Nothing is easier to prove than this fact. " Know you not . . . that the Holy Spirit dwelleth within you ?" " Your members are the temples of the Holy Ghost." " We are marked, and bear within us the pledge of our salvation, the Spirit." " We are participators of the Spirit."

Thus speaks the Apostle, and he returns again and again to the same thought.

In the first epistle of St John we read: *In hoc cognovimus quoniam in eo maneamus, et ipse in nobis, quoniam de Spiritu suo dedit nobis*—" In this we know that we abide in him, and he in us, because he hath given us of his Spirit."†

The Fathers vie with each other in insisting on this same truth. All the great theologians lay stress on it. St Bonaventure declares that those who deny it are in error. " Man can only be pleasing to God in as much as he receives the Holy Spirit, the

* The best works to consult on this special point are the following: Père Meschier: *Le Don de la Pentecôte ;* Cardinal Manning: *The Internal Mission of the Holy Ghost.*

† 1 John iv 13.

uncreated gift. All those who have an exact idea of what is meant by sanctifying grace acknowledge that the Holy Spirit, the *uncreated* gift, dwells truly in the souls of the just. And if any man think otherwise he should be looked upon as a heretic."

And, finally, we have the no less emphatic assurance of St Thomas on the same point.

Moreover, the question has been settled, once for all, by the Council of Trent. It is beyond doubt that grace includes a *created* element, supernatural faculties which enable us to perform supernatural acts. But that the Holy Spirit—*ipsissima persona Spiritus Sancti**—accompanies this created gift is no less energetically affirmed by the Church. The Holy Spirit is not given in the same measure to all Christians who are in a state of grace, but all receive it in an equally true sense.

" It need hardly be said," says Fr. Ramière very truly,† " that this presence of the divine Spirit within the justified soul is altogether different from that which results from the divine immensity by which the Three Persons of the Holy Trinity are everywhere present, even in hell. The Son of God is likewise infinitely and everywhere present, but that does not hinder us from adoring him in a special manner in the holy Eucharist, for we know that he is there present in a special manner—that is, he is there in order to give himself to us. Thus by grace the Holy Spirit is within us, in order to unite himself to us, and to sanctify us.

" This presence is peculiar, and independent in some ways of the first. Suarez explains this by saying that if—which is impossible—the divine immensity did not render the Holy Spirit present within us, he would be brought there by grace. We can picture the poorest man living beside vast wealth without his proximity making him any the

* Cornelius à Lapide.   † *Divinisation*, p. 246.

richer. What makes wealth is not proximity, but possession. Such is the difference between the just and the sinful soul. Sinners, and even the damned, have near them, and even within them, infinite spiritual wealth. Yet they remain in their poverty, because this wealth does not belong to them, while the Christian who is in a state of grace possesses within him the Holy Spirit, and with that spirit, a plenitude of celestial graces, like a treasure of which he is already the proprietor, and on which he can draw without limit."

This is the meaning of the *dulcis hospes animae* (sweet guest of the soul) in the *Veni Sancte Spiritus* for the feast of Pentecost, for the Holy Spirit does, in very truth, delight to take up this abode within our hearts.

But do we, on our side, delight in this thought, that the Holy Spirit is the Guest of our souls ?

Poor " sweet guest "! Is it in sarcasm that the liturgy thus describes you ? You are indeed the guest of our souls, but how many of us give any heed to you ? Can it be that your presence is a gift without any value whatsoever ? No—for you are the *Holy* Spirit, the Spirit which dwells in the Father and in the Son, or, better, the Spirit of the Father and of the Son.

Can it be that in the vast encampment of the soul, amid the stir and the bustle of the arrival and departure of troops with convoys and baggage, there is no lodging for the great captain ?

No. We take it for granted that the soul is in a state of grace. Very well. It follows that the Spirit resides there, and has his dwelling within it. How comes it, then, that there is no guard of honour—at least a simple platoon ? Is it because the Spirit wishes to remain *incognito ?* Not at all. There is nothing he desires so much as to be recognized, saluted by all who pass by, surrounded, and feasted. How few Christians, however, even among the best, try to satisfy this desire ?

" If there is one thing that is to our shame, one thing which ought to cast us down with our faces in the dust, it is this: that we live all the day long as if there were no Holy Ghost, as if we were like the Ephesians who, when the Apostle asked them if they had received the Holy Ghost since they believed, said: ' We have not so much as heard whether there be a Holy Ghost.' "*

Can it be that it is not worth considering, or that there exists any more important question, or any which better merits our constant and most earnest attention ? Is not the Holy Ghost uncreated love, the bourne of the Holy Trinity, " the limit of that which is without limit, the bounds of that which is without bounds ?" Is he not, in the beautiful words of the liturgy, *Spiritus Creator*, the author, not only of the first creation, but also of the second, since it is to him that we owe the supernatural life which was restored to humanity in general, by the fact of his overshadowing of our Lady, the supernatural life which is given back to each of us when he comes to us in baptism ?

Yet, somehow, we never give it a thought ! What a fine excuse ! " I have no time to think about the most essential thing of all !"

When an important personage, an earthly sovereign, pays even a flying visit to a town, the people in that town think of nothing else. How much thought do we spare for the King of Heaven who comes to make his home in our hearts ? As a matter of fact, we do not think anything at all about it ! St Paul, on whose authority we may safely rely, speaks of devotion to the Holy Ghost as anything but an adventitious affair, to be taken

* Manning: *The Internal Mission of the Holy Ghost*, p. 20. London: Burns Oates and Washbourne, Ltd.

or left. He supplies us, on the contrary, with a complete chart, which we will study, on the subject of our duties towards this *dulcis hospes*.

First of all, of course, we must not be in a state of mortal sin. *Spiritum nolite extinguere*. Extinguish not the divine Light, either in your own souls, or, by scandal, in the souls of others. To expel the Spirit, to banish him either from ourselves or from others, is the most supreme insult we can offer him. Moreover, besides insulting the Spirit, we may cause him grief: *Ipsi vero afflixerunt Spiritum Sanctum ejus*. They have afflicted the Holy Spirit, says Isaias; and St Paul gives the early Christians an example of the way in which they may do this. *Omnis sermo malus ex ore vestro non procedat, et nolite contristare Spiritum Sanctum*. Avoid all wounding, or bad words, afflict not the Spirit. Moreover, it is certain that every venial sin we commit grieves the Spirit, who accompanies our every step, and is the witness of all our words, all our actions, thoughts, and desires.

There is also another, and higher, command. This Spirit whom we may insult (by mortal sin) or grieve (by venial sin) may find his inspirations resisted. *Vos semper Spiritui Sancto resistitis**— "You always resist the Holy Ghost." How many times does the " sweet guest of the soul " incite us gently to do good, and how many times his efforts are in vain, because we, on our part, fail, or refuse, to correspond. The Holy Spirit is constantly calling and stimulating us. Where are we, when he is speaking ? If we are not actually absent, do we really give ear to him ? What sort of answer do we make to his invitations ?

This purely *negative* charter is far from exhausting the list of our duties towards the Holy Ghost,

* Acts iv 10.

as St Paul understands them; as a right understanding of what is meant by a state of grace
prescribes; and as intelligent piety requires.

Here, as elsewhere, the *positive* is the more fertile
point of view.

The presence of the Holy Spirit within us not
only invites us to *refrain from doing*, but it also
incites us *to do*. To do what? To find more room
in our hearts for our divine Guest; to seek, by every
means, to profit by the wonder of his presence; and
to become more and more, day by day, more closely
united to him in friendship and in love.

The Spirit within us is a *living*, and therefore a
moving Spirit. It is we ourselves who determine
the limits of his activity. He, on his side, desires
to give himself, and to unite himself to us as closely
as possible. But we lay down the measurements
of the space we allot to the Spirit of Love in our
hearts. He is the " guest." We are the " hosts."
His movements depend on ours.

" If you but knew the gift of God," says Mgr. Gay,
" and the value, the importance of the smallest
interior illumination; the lightest touch of the
Holy Ghost; the smallest favourable opportunity!
If you only knew that God is there, and how he is
offering himself there, how he gives of himself;
and what that involves for you, and for others, and
what are its consequences, in time and eternity!
Ah! who shall teach us the understanding of supernatural things, and a right estimate of these benefits,
the least of which, in the opinion of St Thomas, is
superior to all natural benefits put together?"

What should we be but for his *foreseeing* kindness, which, before we reached the age of reason,
led us to the baptismal font, there to bestow upon
us the *charity of God* [which] *is poured forth in our
hearts by the Holy Ghost;** without his constant

* Rom. v 4.

adjuvant kindness, to which we owe those upliftings
of the soul which every Christian who is in the
habit of examining his conscience remembers with
such joy—inspirations in prayer, strength in such
and such a temptation, encouragement in such and
such circumstances; without his wondrously *patient*
kindness, which, every time we fall, raises us again;
every time we give way to sin, draws us back from
the abyss; every time we treat him with scant
courtesy, shows us yet one more example of his
consideration for us ?

Can we imagine anything more wonderful than
the diligence with which the Holy Spirit strives for
our sanctification ? It is only equalled by the
diligence with which we refuse to co-operate with
him, when, that is, we do not simply pass by on the
other side without as much as a suspicion of this
work of his, or of its wondrous value.

If only we were as ambitious for ourselves as
God is for us !

The most important point, however, is not that the
Spirit gives us his strength, his aspirations, his love.
It is rather that, in addition to all that, *he gives us
himself*. All this means to us we shall presently see.

Some obscure and secret fear hinders us from
recognizing this union between the Holy Spirit and
our souls for what it really is (or, rather, ought to
be)—a union so intimate, says Cornelius à Lapide,
in his *Commentary on the Acts*, that no greater exists.
*Est enim summa unio inter Deum et animam sanctam
quà nullius creaturae purae potest esse major.* And
St Paul declares: *He who is joined to the Lord is
one spirit.**

" In the same way," says Cornelius à Lapide, " the
soul, when it embraces the body, communicates to
it life and breath, in which it was hitherto lacking;
so, too, the Holy Ghost, when he takes a soul to

* 1 Cor. vi 17.

unite himself with it, communicates to it new life, and, what is more, his own life. Literally, he deifies it."*

It is certain that this union between our souls and the Holy Spirit does not mean that he forms one person with us. Having made this reservation, however, we may truly say that, from a certain point of view, this union is closer than that between our body and our soul, " since," observes Fr. Ramière, " the divine Spirit better penetrates the faculties of our soul than our soul penetrates the members of our body. Above all, this union is much more indissoluble. The union between body and soul is so fragile that it is constantly being dissolved. Every instant we lose some part of our substance, until the day comes when our whole body is snatched from us by the irresistible grasp of death. When the Holy Spirit unites himself with a soul nothing, either on earth or in hell, has the power to snatch him from us. Only that soul to whom he unites himself has the power to destroy the divine life within it, by the most dreadful of suicides."†

The Fathers of the Church declare more boldly (and perhaps with greater truth) that the union between the Holy Spirit and the justified soul is so intimate that it constitutes a real marriage. He is, then, not merely the " guest," but the " bridegroom," and some even go so far as to call the soul *Spirita Sancta*—the feminine form of *Spiritus Sanctus*‡—in order to show that the union

* "Sicut anima, dum assumit et quasi osculatur corpus, ipsum exanima animat et vivificat; sic Spiritus Sanctus gratia osculatur animam, eam vivificat, imo deificat" (*In Cant.* I).

† *Divinisation du Chrétien*, p. 233.

‡ See Père Meschier: *Le Don de la Pentecôte*, vol. ii, p. 139.

between the divine Paraclete and the soul which
is free from mortal sin is a union resembling (except
that it is far more beautiful) the union between
man and woman in the sacrament which makes
them one flesh and one soul; a union similar
(though it is non-hypostatic) to the union of
the Word with the sacred Humanity; a union
like that which unites Christ with his Church,
of which we may regard Christian marriage as a
symbol.

In the third book of the life of Blessed Angela of
Foligno we read how one day she went in pilgrimage
to Assisi, to the tomb of St Francis. There she
hears a voice: " Thou hast had recourse to my
servant Francis, but I will make known to thee
another support. I am the Holy Ghost, who am
come to thee, and whose desire it is to give thee
such joy as thou hast not yet tasted. And I
accompany thee: I am present with thee . . . and
I will ever speak with thee . . . and, if thou dost
love me, I will never leave thee. O my spouse, I
love thee. I have established myself within thee.
I take my rest in thee. And do thou, in thy turn,
establish thyself within me, and seek thy rest in
me." Blessed Angela, comparing her sins with these
signal favours, hesitated, and believed she was the
victim of a delusion: " If you are truly the Holy
Ghost you could not speak such words to me.
They are not for me. If it were indeed you my
joy would be so great that I could not bear it
without dying." And he answered: " Am I not
master of my gifts? I give the joy that I desire,
neither more nor less." And the saint ends by
saying: " I cannot describe the joy I felt, above
all when he said to me: ' I am the Holy Ghost,
who dwelleth interiorly with thee.' "

That which the Holy Ghost revealed, by special
favour, to Blessed Angela, is precisely what all

Christians learn from the Church. The Holy Ghost dwells interiorly with us, and he has but one desire —to find in our souls a reciprocation of the sentiments which he is pleased to feel for us.

How closely, indeed, does he unite himself with us! But how closely do we unite ourselves to him? Can it be that we are wanting in intelligence, or heart? Or are we so amazingly ignorant of, or hopelessly blind to, the love of Love itself? How are we to escape from this dilemma?

Some souls, however, more contemplative or more eager to draw closer to God, have more than a suspicion that this is the means to achieve their end. But all at once, and just because more than most people they realize their weakness, they hesitate. They have not the courage to go on. They draw back.

Here is the Holy Ghost offering them a union without parallel—a true marriage—and they feel ashamed to hold out their hands to him, and to give him their hearts. It is not for them! It is too beautiful! Their body, which is but sinful dust, their soul, *ulcus et apostema*, in the strange words of St Ignatius in his meditation on sin—a canker, and an ulcer—at all events the grave of God's gifts! And so, while they are animated by the ardent desire to unite themselves with the divine Guest, they feel so much reluctance, looking at themselves, that they refuse to believe *practically* in the reality of the divine offer.

The *touch me not* of Christ to Mary Magdalen echoes in their ears, and they remember the exclamation of Peter when he sees Jesus about to wash his feet, and that of Elizabeth when she sees Mary coming to visit her. *Tu mihi?* You, to come to my dwelling! *Unde hoc . . . ut veniat?* Whence comes this marvellous thing?

The question, however, is not to know whether it is too *beautiful*, but rather to know if it is *true*.

Is it true that the Holy Ghost dwells within our souls, and desires thus to unite himself with us? Yes, it is perfectly true. I have nothing to do with it. It is a fact. I am free to consider this fact extraordinary, incomprehensible, or unheard-of. Nevertheless, since it is true, I must bow my head, I must accept it.

Now, the fact remains, and cannot be ignored.

It follows, then, that it would be extraordinary, incomprehensible, and unheard-of if I, on my part, did not seek to penetrate this mystery, to persuade myself of its truth, and to live in the light of it.

" Whatever graces may be ours," says M. Olier,* " we are still the same earthenware vessels, still the same miserable nonentities, and nothing more. *Habemus thesaurum istum in vasis fictilibus.* The elements of bread and wine," he adds, " have no call to glorify themselves because of the graces they enclose, or the benefits which the holy Eucharist works in our souls, because they are not the cause, but only the thin, fragile covering, for all they approach the divinity so near.

" Thus it is with the holiest souls, and those most filled with the Holy Ghost. They are but the shell, or covering, which in a very short while will spoil and decay. And just as the Body and Blood of our Lord cease to be present under elements which are in a state of decay, so, too, at the first sign of corruption or impurity, the Holy Ghost departs, and leaves these poor vessels of ours to their destruction.

Judge by that whether a soul, because it receives such precious favours as the sacraments, and

* See his *Life*, published by Lebel, Versailles, 1818, pp. 498-499.

because, like the bread and wine, it bears our Lord within it, or because, like the consecrated oil and the balm of Confirmation, it bears within it the Holy Ghost, has any cause to glorify itself, or to believe itself to be more than it was formerly. Should it not, on the contrary, fear greatly lest our Lord should withdraw himself, not finding it pure enough to be his dwelling-place ?"

And, while we are speaking of Holy Communion, is the presence of the Holy Ghost—and of the whole Trinity—within our hearts any more incomprehensible, any more extraordinary, and more unheard-of, than that of our Lord's presence in the holy Eucharist ?

How marvellous is the marriage (writers often employ this word in connection with the *union* of the soul with our Lord in Holy *Communion*) between the Christian who approaches the altar and Jesus Christ who comes down to dwell within his heart !

Why, then, if this mystery does not shock or repel us, should we hesitate at the idea of that other presence of God which is a result of our being in a state of grace ?

St Bernard goes further. In face of the objection: " I shall never dare to enter into such familiarity . . . God in me ? No !" he answers:

"What gives you pause is respect (*reverentia*); and in the word respect (*vereor*) there is included the idea of fear. You forget that love is love, not reverence. To fear, to be amazed, to wonder—that is to reverence; but that has nothing to do with love. Where love is, every other feeling disappears. He who loves, loves. He loves, and nothing else. The bride and the bridegroom. Now here, is not the Holy Ghost the bridegroom of the soul, one who loves, and no more; better still, love itself ? God exacts that, as God, he should be feared; as father, that he should be honoured; bridegroom, that he should be loved. . . . When God loves, he wishes nothing except to be loved. . . . Undoubtedly there are degrees in love. The love of the bride is the highest. There is nothing beyond it.

" Now the union of the Holy Ghost with the soul is a union of this order, and of the highest possible degree. It is a union, not of two bodies, but of two *spirits*, in the emphatic words of St Paul— *qui adhaeret Deo, unus spiritus est.* He who is joined to the Lord is one Spirit."*

And when the soul still takes refuge in humility, and excuses itself, saying: " I shall never be able to love enough. Can one wrestle with a giant ?

* St Bernard: *In cantic.* S. lxxxiii. The passage runs as follows:

" Nec verendum ne disparitas personarum claudicare in aliquo faciat convenientiam voluntatum, quia amor reverentiam nescit. Ab amando quippe amor, non ad honorando denominatur. Honoret sane qui horret, qui stupet, qui metuit, qui miratur; vacant haec omnes penes amantem. Amor, ubi venerit, exteros in se omnes traducit et captivat effectus. Propterea, qui amat, amat et aliud novit nihil. . . . Sponsus et Sponsa sunt. . . . Iste sponsus, non modo amans sed Amor est. . . . Exigit Deus timeri ut Dominus, honorari ut Pater, et ut sponsus, amari. Quid in his praestat, quid eminet ? Nempe amor. . . . Amo quia amo, amo ut amem. Magna res amor. . . . Cum amat Deus, non aliud vult quam amari. Magna res amor, sed sunt in eo gradus. Sponsa in summo stat. Felix cui tantae suavi atis complexum experiri donatum est ! Quod non est alius quam amor sanctus et castus, amor intimus qui non in carne una sed uno plane in spiritu duos jungat, duos faciat jam non duos sed unum, Paulo ita dicente ! Qui adhaeret Deo, unus spiritus est."

The union of the bride and the bridegroom in the *Canticle of Canticles* symbolizes more generally the mystical union. All that St Bernard says here, with the exception of the experimental knowledge (*experiri*), and of the sweetness (*suavitatis*) tasted in this union is fundamentally and substantially true of the union of the soul which is in a state of grace with the Holy Ghost.

How can I love as much as I am loved ? Must I not give up the attempt ?" " No," replies the saint. " Undoubtedly, the creature loves less. But provided that the soul loves without reserve, is anything wanting, there where all is given ?"*

St John of the Cross completes the explanation, and gives the ultimate and most profound reason—that the soul can love Love enough, because, in her, it is Love who loves.†

Here, then, is the desired proportion, the seemingly impossible equality. If the soul were not fortified, doubled, even to a hundredfold, in her capacity for love, the necessary equation could never be established. But if the love with which she loves is the love of God himself, everything is explained.

Now this, in fact, is the case, and St Fulgentius explains it in these admirable words: " In order to love God the heart of man will not suffice. He must have the heart of God. What, can we then love God with God's heart ? Yes, for ' the charity of God is poured forth in our hearts by the Holy Ghost which is given to us,' and since we can only love God by the Holy Ghost, am I not right in saying to you: ' Let us love God with God's heart ' ?"

* "Etsi minus diligit creatura quoniam minor est; tamen si ex tota se diligit, nihil deest ubi totum est." Id., *ibid.*

† St John of the Cross, *The Dark Night of the Soul*, bk. ii, ch. xiii. We have already seen the explanation given by St Paul: " God hath sent forth his Spirit, the Spirit of his Son, into our hearts, whereby we cry, Abba, Father." We have here the same argument. We have made some attempt to develop this beautiful and fundamental dogma in the review *L'Apôtre Laïque*, October, 1918.

CHAPTER IV

WITH THE WHOLE TRINITY

DEVOTION to the Father, devotion to the Son, and devotion to the Holy Ghost, all of whom are present within us as long as we are in a state of grace, may be regarded from a great many different angles, according to the spiritual aspirations and the different attractions experienced by each individual soul.

Hence that widely-differing character which is found among the various souls who give themselves to a life of piety, and which wrung from David such a cry of admiration: *Mirabilis Deus in sanctus suis ;* God is wonderful in those among whom he inhabits.*

Instead of concentrating their attention on the presence of one or other of the divine Persons who abide within the soul, or on such and such a point of view in connection with either one of the Three, certain people find it more useful and congenial to meditate on the whole Trinity.

" Christ, very God and very Man, as truly Man as he is truly God, born of the Father in the splendours of Eternity, has, in some sort, engendered us on Calvary. Becoming by his sacrifice the chief of all humanity, he makes us participators in the divine life which he has received from his Father. On our natural life he grafts his supernatural life, and he communicates to us his divine existence. Dwelling in very truth within us, he is necessarily inseparable from his Father, and from the Holy Spirit.

* Psalm lxvii 36.

" Within our souls, the Father is engendering his Son, and the Holy Spirit is proceeding from the Father and from the Son. All the mysteries, all the operations, all the love, all the beatitude of the Most Holy Trinity are thus accomplished, and abide in us.

" Such are the sublime realities of the state of grace. . . ."*

Father Lessius, whose beautiful book, *On the Divine Names*, is so well known, is one of those who have studied most deeply the mystery of the adorable Trinity, and we see that his personal piety derived its nourishment from the practice of meditating on the presence of God within the soul:

" Lord, I pray thee, draw my heart to thee, *in the interior of my soul*. *There*, far from the noise of the world, far from the importunate cares which overwhelm us, I would dwell near to thee, to enjoy thee, to love thee, to venerate thee, and to hearken to thy voice. To *thee* will I recount the sorrows of my life of exile. *There* shall I find, near to thee, the necessary consolations ! Grant that I may never forget thy presence *within me*, O thou light and sweetness of my soul ! May I never forget thee; may the eyes of my soul always and everywhere be fixed on thee."

The *Souvenirs* of Sister Elizabeth of the Trinity are one long recital of what devotion to " the Three " can—and ought to—be. We have already given evidence on this point, and we will content ourselves now with giving two extracts from the prayer she habitually used. Nothing more dogmatic, and at the same time poetical; more exact, and at the same time elevated, can possibly be imagined:

" O my God, the Trinity whom I adore, help me to forget myself entirely, to establish myself in

* Pauline Reynolds, vol. ii, ch. iii, par. 4.

you, motionless and tranquil as if my soul were already in eternity! Grant that nothing may trouble my peace, or cause me to leave you, my Immovable God, but that each moment may carry me further and further into the depths of your Mystery.

"Pacify my soul, make of it your heaven, your beloved dwelling, and the place of your repose. Grant that I may never leave you there alone, but that I am to be there entirely, in all-lively faith, all-adoring, and entirely abandoned to your creative action."

The prayer thus begins, and it finishes as follows:

"O my Three, my All, my Beatitude, infinite Solitude, Immensity in which I lose myself, I give myself entirely to you, as your prey. Bury yourself in me, that I may bury myself in you, until the day comes that I shall go to contemplate the depths of your greatness, in your Light" (November 21, 1904).

It is quite a mistake to imagine that it is necessary to be a nun, like Sister Elizabeth, endowed with extraordinary graces, or a scholar, deeply learned in theology, in order to pray thus. Any person who has a right understanding of what is meant by this mystery of the Indwelling, is capable of devotion to "the Three" who abide within our souls; for this is no extraordinary devotion, set aside for the few. The dogma, and the devotion which arises out of it, are intended for all Christians alike.

Take the example of the student Pierre Poyet, a young man no different from his companions, except in his devotion to his faith. He loved to take the opportunity of the usual morning prayer to withdraw within himself, and to commune with the divine Guest of his soul: "Let us put ourselves in the presence of God, and adore him." Where was God more truly present than in the heart of this young man of twenty, who was in a state of grace? Every aspiration of his youthful soul was centred on this great idea—the Indwelling of the Trinity in the soul.

" Has God the place he ought to have within you?" he writes to a school friend; and in the rule of life he made for himself we find this resolution: " *To have a soul tormented by the magic of the divine absence.*" This is the sin above all else to be dreaded, because it means banishing God from our hearts. More than all else, we must strive to remain in a state of grace, because it ensures *the divine presence* within us.

Which of us cannot imitate—or strive to imitate —this young student, in his faith, and his desire? Undoubtedly for us, gross and material-minded as we are, it means a considerable effort. " The smallness of our ego," says Pascal, profoundly, " hides from us the sight of the Infinite."

From the moment, nevertheless, that we begin to realize what we lose by neglecting to meditate on the wealth we carry within our souls, we must surely feel an ambition to achieve, at whatever cost, and as far as in us lies, communion within the unseen Guest of our souls, so that we may no longer be said to pass by the greatest of all wonders without being aware of its existence, or to possess such wealth, and yet to ignore its use.

We have purposely omitted, in this study, all controversial questions, and all those points in connection with the subject which, while they are profitable to students of theology, are of no great use to us when we kneel before the tabernacle, or commune with our own souls.

We will therefore confine ourselves here to

mentioning two points which will meet a difficulty, or answer an objection, which may possibly arise.

Does the Holy Ghost, in this mystery of your sanctification, play a separate part, which is not shared to the same degree, by the Father and the Son ? According to certain writers, who rely on trustworthy historical tradition, handed down in particular by the Greek Fathers, and especially by St Cyril of Alexandria, it is *by* the Holy Ghost that the Father and the Son abide within us. There are, as it were, two stages, not in the chronological but in the logical order, and of what is called formal causality. The Holy Spirit, by baptism, takes possession of our souls. This is the first stage.

Thanks to the privilege of *circumincession*, by which there where the Spirit is found the Father and Son are likewise present, immediately after the coming of the Holy Spirit the Father and the Son become equally present.

That is the first point, and the second is this:

In what manner, precisely, is produced within us the union of God with us, and of us with him ? We say: God is present. He lives, dwells within me. The *fact* is certain. It is a dogma of the Church. The question is *how ?*

No scholar, to our knowledge, has dealt with this question more deeply than Père Jouvene, in his *De vita deiformi*.

We take up this book; we sit down to read; we devour page after page; we finish it; and we close it, feeling rather disconcerted. Habitation, possession, divine life, intimacy, familiarity—all this is packed into a few seemingly inadequate explanations, and a few short formulas.

We are wrong to be surprised.
The question *how* cannot be answered to our

satisfaction. We do not understand, or, at least, we do not *sufficiently* understand it. But, when we come to think of it, is there anything to surprise us in that ? Is it not, on the other hand, what we should expect ? If I could understand it, would it be such a great mystery, after all ? And what is more, is it anything new for us to find that we do not understand God's ways ? Moreover, if I do fail to grasp this mystery, is there not still that in it which arouses my deepest admiration, and which, if I do but wish it, will sanctify my soul beyond my dearest desires ?

It is not as if it were the *only* mystery connected with our faith which escapes our comprehension.

Take the Eucharist. Do we know exactly what takes place in transubstantiation ? Would it benefit my piety to any great extent to make an exhaustive study of the various systems—adduction, reproduction, simple conversion, and so on ? Yet—what is more certain than the fact itself ?

Is there any danger, moreover, that, for want of instruction, I should over-estimate my spiritual wealth, and exaggerate the work of sanctification within my soul which is a result of the divine Indwelling ?

No. There is no danger, for I have a standard by which I can judge of this matter. I know that I must stop short at anything bordering on pantheism. God is God, and I am I. I know that my union with him is not an hypostatic union—in other words, of the same nature as that between the sacred Humanity and the Word.

That is enough, and within these limits the dogma of the life of God within us, by grace, is surely great enough, and beautiful enough, to satisfy the deepest aspirations of our hearts.

BOOK V

THE PRACTICE OF INTIMACY WITH GOD WITHIN US

W E have now seen what a treasure is within our possession. This treasure will be ours, indeed, if only we strive—

(1) To desire it;
(2) To protect it;
(3) To conquer it.

CHAPTER I

TO DESIRE OUR TREASURE

WE read in the life of M. Olier that he often heard a gentle but insistent voice murmur in his ear the words: *Divine life, divine life.* After his second conversion, when he made an act of total surrender to God, " his existence was, as it were, a *solemnity.* The ugliness of the appearances melted into nothing before the grandeur of the realities. His whole life is expressed in this prayer which he addressed to God: ' May your light be the single light which shall guide me, and make me see all things as they are in themselves.' "*

* E. Hello: *Le Siècle*, p. 400. M. Olier, in his turn, gives us a portrait of Père de Condren: " What he outwardly appeared was but the outside or the shell. Within, he was an entirely different person, resembling the inner life of Jesus Christ himself, so that we might say it was Jesus Christ

Are we in need of such a voice as that which spoke to M. Olier, to induce us to adopt the two words, *Life divine*, as our watchword? No. We have but to remember what our faith teaches us. We need, however, " a slight touch of clairvoyance," as Mother Cécile de Solesmes calls it in her *Spiritual Life and Prayer*, in order to be able " diligently to cultivate our baptism."

When the patriarch Jacob saw in a vision that mysterious ladder which reached from earth, and the angels which descended and ascended it, he awoke, filled with dread, crying: " Indeed, God is in this place, and I knew it not. How terrible is this place ! This is no other than the house of God, and this the gate of heaven." " So would it be with us," says Cardinal Manning, " if we were to wake up and be conscious that God the Holy Ghost is about us, that he encompasses us behind and before, that he is within us . . . that he is all ear to hear every breathing of our heart, that he is all eye to see every thought that flits across our imagination; that our whole being is open before him."*

Unhappily the majority of men live as if they did not possess such a thing as a soul, while even among those who have at least some idea of what it means, and of the possibility of its being saved, or damned for all eternity, the greater part live as if God did not dwell in very truth within them.

"They are unconscious of the divine presence: I do not mean in the world around them, because it is an axiom of the human reason that God is everywhere. . . . I am speaking now of the

living in Père de Condren, rather than Père de Condren living in Jesus Christ. He was like the Host in our tabernacles. Outwardly, one saw the accidents, and the appearances. Inwardly, there was Jesus Christ."

* *Internal Mission of the Holy Ghost*, p. 27.

internal presence of God the Holy Ghost working
in the soul. Even they who are Christians in faith
and in spiritual light, who are conscious and are
continually saying that they have a soul at stake,
even they, too, live without an habitual daily sense
that they are never alone: that as the soul is in the
body, so God is in the soul. Now this is the
truth. . . .*

" We are, without being aware of it, the Paradise
of God. We must think and act in such a manner
that God may, in his turn, be our Paradise."†

This, ambitious as it may seem, should be the
ambition of every baptized Christian.

Cardinal Newman has defined the true Christian
as a man absorbed by a feeling of the presence
of God within him, living in this thought that God
is there, in the depths of his heart; a man whose
conscience is illuminated by God to such an extent
that he lives in the habitual impression that each
one of his troubles, and every fibre of his moral life,
his every motive and desire, is spread before the
Almighty.

Alas! if that is to be our standard, how few
" true Christians " do we find amongst us!

" In the hearts of many," complained our Lord
to Benigna Consolata Ferrero, a Visitation nun at
Como, " I am, as it were, an unprofitable treasure.
They possess me, because they are in a state of
grace, but they do not turn it to account. Do thou
make up for this."

What can we do, in order that we may turn to
account this presence of God within our souls?

---

* *Internal Mission of the Holy Ghost*, p. 34. Manning is
here speaking of knowledge gained, not by experience, but
by faith.

† Sertillanges: *La Vie en Présence de Dieu* (*Revue des
Jeunes*, May 10, 1918, p. 546).

First of all, of course, we must make it the subject of frequent meditations.* It is obvious that if we deliberately and courageously try every morning—or as often as we are able—to fix our minds on the centre of our souls, there where our Treasure is to be found, we shall soon, from mere force of habit, as well as by the grace of God, become spontaneously and naturally familiar with the idea of God's presence within us.

" Men live on the surface of their souls, without ever penetrating their profound content. If only we knew how to withdraw within ourselves, to read our own souls, and to understand," says Elizabeth Leseur in her *Journal* (p. 298).

" God dwells within us. What sort of reception do we give such a guest ? I am confounded by the thought that he has no sooner entered my abode than I turn my back on him, and leave him, on some trifling errand," says Pauline Reynolds.

We purposely invoke the testimony of two women who lived in the world, one all her life, and the other until she was fifty-seven, when she became a Carmelite nun.

People are far too much inclined to suppose that the doctrine of the Indwelling of the Holy Ghost in the soul is a matter which concerns only those who are called to embrace the religious life. The fact is that people living in the world are so often carried away by the excitement of life around them, that they cannot be persuaded to practise the silence which is necessary in order to hear the mysterious voice of the divine, speaking within their souls.

God is a hidden God—*Deus absconditus*. He

* To those who are attracted by this subject we would mention our little *Imitation : Living with God*, which is a collection of short reflections suitable in order to grasp the meaning of the spiritual treasures hidden within our souls.

will only reveal himself in tranquillity.   In noise we shall seek him in vain.   *Non in commotione Dominus.*

" I feel," says Pauline Reynolds, " that the first thing required of me is silence in accordance with the words of Tauler: the Father has but one word, his Word, and his Son.   He speaks this word in an eternal silence; and it is in silence that the soul receives it and understands it."

And she continues: " Silence, then, O my soul, in order to hear God.   Silence to receive the Word; silence in order that he may have speech with thee, make himself understood by thee, dwell with thee. Silence and prayer."

Unfortunately, as Elizabeth Leseur says, and as we all know, silence is the one thing in which our generation is lacking.

Père Gratry tried one day to picture to himself what would become of the world if everyone could be induced to reap that silence for one half-hour of which we read in the Scriptures—if they could be persuaded to meet together, to meditate in silence, for half an hour, on their eternal destiny.

What would be the result ?   I think we can guess !   Meanwhile, where are we to find that solitude in which the God who is hidden within our souls is to be found ?

Renan's grandson, Psichari, owed his conversion to the long months he spent in the desert.   Noise is a disintegrating and corrupting influence, but " the desert is a holy place.   Our Lord went down into the desert, and in the desert hundreds of religious have learnt holiness.   I mean that Thebaids still exist, and that earnest souls are not wanting to contemplate the word of God."

Thebaids still exist.   The desert is never lacking to the souls whom " vast spaces " do not terrify, and who are spurred on by the desire to explore them, because they suspect, in advance, towards what discoveries the caravan of their souls will set forth.   Wheresoever they may find themselves, these enlightened and courageous souls know how to find the silence they are in need of.   " There will always be enough solitude," it has been said, " for those who are worthy of it."*

The desire to become better acquainted with this mystery will engender a love of prayer and meditation; and, in its turn, the habit of prayer and meditation will engender an increasing eagerness to penetrate more and more into the depths of the interior closet of the soul.

Every day, then, we shall discover more riches, till we are inspired to cry out, with the Apostles: *It is good for us to be here.   Here will we dwell. Here will we pitch our tent.*

In uttering this cry, moreover, we shall but echo that of God himself, who, in his mercy, having gazed on the fragile shelter of man's heart, decided to make it his favoured dwelling, and a substitute for Paradise: *Bonum est nos hic esse*—it is good for us to be here, said the Holy Trinity. *Mansionem apud eum faciemus*—Here will we make our dwelling.

We can understand, therefore, the ambitions which certain souls will cherish.   One will resolve to be ever " the little one busy with the great Forgotten."   " What a host of things there are to tell each other," she says, " when two people always live together; when they love each other utterly, and when one of the two is God."   And she makes this resolution: to profit in a special manner by silence,

* We seize this opportunity to urge the practice, not only of daily meditation, but also of retreat, and especially of enclosed retreats.

since it is, as it were, a sacrament, for he is always there.*

Yes, God is always there, but we cannot always be there too.   If it were so, the world would be heaven.   All we can do is to try to " be there " as often as we possibly can.

In the case of many souls a sort of gulf is fixed between the time spent on prayer and the time spent in the workaday world.

How often do we find this to be the case, even among pious and fervent souls.   They will spend a few moments, more or less, in prayer, or even in meditation or mental prayer, every morning, and then they will proceed to spend the rest of the day without a thought of God.   Their life is, as it were, divided into two.   They spend a few minutes thinking about God, but for the rest of the time they forget him.   Yet, if they would, they could surely find the time.   The day is long enough !

" I resolve not to confine Jesus to my communions and my prayers," says Pauline Reynolds,

---

* This programme is indeed that of all the saints.   The biographer of St Gregory the Great sums up his life in these two words: *secum vivebat*.   He was an *interior* man.   St Jerome, too, writes to Eustochium: *Semper te cubiculi tui secreta custodiant, semper tecum Sponsus ludat intrinsecus. Oras, loqueris ad Sponsum ; legis, ille tibi loquitur*, etc.: " Shut the door of your cell behind you, and live an interior life there where dwells the Bridegroom at home with you." We need not impress upon the reader that leading an interior life does not mean indulging in habits of scrupulous introspection, of perpetual and morbid brooding over our small   shortcomings,   or   of   constant   and   quite   useless dwelling on the past.   Some souls are only too much inclined to such practices as these, which are far removed from real devotion.   Such feverish introspection, and such endless examinations of conscience are as fruitless, and even as dangerous, as the habit of recollection which we have striven to explain, and that the object of which is not ourselves, but God, is fruitful.

" but to say to him: ' I will not let you go.' "
Every one of us should make the same resolution.

" This habit of prayer on the slightest occasion,"
adds Pauline Reynolds, " helps us to realize the
nearness of the invisible world." We will go
further. We will say that without such a habit
of prayer on the slightest occasion, it is impossible
to realize the nearness of the invisible world. And,
furthermore, until we do realize it, we shall never
be in a position to lead an interior life.

When Martha bids Mary come, because the
Master is there, and is waiting for her, it is at no
fixed hour. With us, the Master is ever there, and
ever, as St Paul says, calling us. *Magister adest
et vocat.* Yes. He calls—but do we always answer ?
Yet he calls each one of us. *Vocat te.*

" It was at the sixth hour," the Gospel tells us,
when Jesus spoke with the woman of Samaria at
the well. With us, our Lord is present at six o'clock
—eleven o'clock—one o'clock—all hours ! All day
long, all our lives long, he is waiting. It is always
time to go to him. We envy the Samaritan woman,
perhaps, but that woman is none other than ourselves. It is six o'clock. Jesus is standing by
Jacob's Well, waiting for us. The edge of the well
on which he leans and waits is the threshold of our
hearts. He cannot do without us. There, where
he is, he wishes us to be. And it is not there, at
the door of our hearts, that he has his dwelling,
but in the very depths of our hearts. There is his
chosen sanctuary. We cannot always be kneeling
before the altar, so he makes his tabernacle in our
hearts. From within this tabernacle he invites us,
and since he desires nothing so much as to be
desired, he seeks to discover whether or not we feel
the need of him in our lives.

How few souls thirst for anything beyond the
satisfaction of their material needs ! One is tempted

to say of most of us that we have all we want; and yet—what strange creatures we must be, to be satisfied with *nothing!* Only those who have caught a glimpse of the Master as he passes by will ask: Where has the Messiah his dwelling? Only those who already love him can say, as St. Mary Magdalen said to him whom she took to be the gardener, on that Easter morning: Where have they laid him? Moreover, those who seek for him as she sought have already found him.

St Francis Xavier was astonished at the number of traders in pepper and spice he came across in the East. Many of us, too, have marvelled at the hardships endured by the gold-prospectors in Alaska. How is it, we ask ourselves, that more people are not to be found who are seeking after the one pearl beyond price, in order that, as far as they can, they may enjoy its constant possession?

" One trembles," says Psichari, " to write in the presence of the Holy Trinity." Before each one of our actions, let us, like him, pause, and call to mind the presence of him who dwells within us. " I have no church," says another soldier, " but I withdraw with myself, where God is."* We read, too, of a certain admiral, lately deceased, who strove constantly to remind himself of the presence of God within him, in order to lead an interior life.

" He is within me, and I do not heed him. He has me in his heart, and I can scarcely keep him

---

* The practice of an interior life is a source of strength and consolation to those souls who, for one reason or another, are unable frequently to go to Communion. As Sister Elizabeth of the Trinity writes, in a letter to her sister: " You are deprived of receiving our Lord as often as you would like. I understand what a sacrifice it is; but you must remember that your beloved has need of sacraments in order to visit you. Communicate with him all day long, for he dwells within your soul!" As we have seen, however, this thought should in nowise diminish our desire to receive our Lord in Holy Communion.

for a moment in my mind," says Père de Gonnelieu, in his very helpful book, *La Présence de Dieu.*

Yet every baptized person ought surely to follow the advice which Père Sertillanges puts so happily—" to make of everything an exaltation, a prayer, a ritual, a saving action, an act of love; to make the house an oratory, and the table, the bed, the carpenter's bench, the office, the wash-tub, the house-wife's or the servants' oven, an altar; to make life, from morning till night, and from night till morning, sleep, rest, amusement, conversation, as well as work and prayer, a religious ceremony, an act of eternity in time—this is a Christian thought. And it is the effort of all those who really understand it. Moreover, we shall only be Christians in proportion as we adapt ourselves to it."

" To make of everything an exaltation." We have here the same idea of which we spoke in the beginning of the chapter, in speaking of M. Olier—" his life was like a solemnity."

It is indeed one thing to possess God by grace within our souls, and another to let every fibre of our being become penetrated by the grace of God. It is one thing to be *habitually* in a state of grace, and another to live in an *ever-active* state of grace.

Did we say ever-active ? Can we hope to live in the constant thought of God's presence ?

No—and in order to avoid scruples and mis-understandings we must make quite sure on this point. Without the gift of rare and gratuitous graces, it is a psychological impossibility for us constantly to think of God. We must take " always," then, to mean that as far as in us lies we will strive to forget our divine Guest as seldom as possible, and that we will seek him diligently, not as a matter of duty, but from the natural inclination of our hearts.

Moreover, if this seems too little, we must remember that " the anxiety we feel because he is not always present testifies in itself to his presence within us."*

CHAPTER II

PROTECTING OUR TREASURE

Depositum custodi. Jealously guard the deposit. A simple desire to live an interior life is not enough to increase the bond between us and the treasure we bear within us. A jewel so precious cannot but excite envy. We must take endless precautions against losing it.

The soldier in the trenches is not content simply to wait for the attack. To guard against being surprised he barricades himself with barbed wire, and uses every conceivable weapon of defence.

So should our soul, which is the casket wherein God is to be found, keep jealous guard over its treasures, refusing, like Tarcisius, to surrender them to the rabble in the market-place.

A certain prince and subject of the Roman Emperor used to wear constantly round his neck a small gold plate on which were engraved the words: "*Remember that thou art Caesar's*"! We can go further. We can say: " *Remember that Caesar is thine*"! And this is a thought which carries with it certain responsibilities.

We have no choice but to live among our fellow-creatures. The author of the *Imitation*, speaking, no doubt, from experience, judges " the world" somewhat harshly. " Every time I have gone amongst men," he says, recalling the words of Seneca, " I have come back less of a man than

* Baudrand: *L'Ame intérieure*, p. 199.

before." We may go further. We may say: " I came back with less of *God* within me than before— less penetrated by the presence within me of the divine Master."

We should therefore avoid all unnecessary amusements, all useless occupations, all needless friendships or intimacies, and all superfluous society. Mark that we have nothing to say about what is necessary. Neither are we speaking of what is harmful. We merely say *unnecessary*—and that means a great deal.

" Your society," says St Paul, " should be with God, with Christ Jesus." *Societas vestra cum Christo, in Deo*. He mentions no other. Thus our " conversation " will be " in heaven," for no other sort should take place within souls which, as we have seen, may be called *churches* and *tabernacles*.

Moreover, if charity, the duties of our calling or zeal, oblige or invite us to renounce the interior life, let us see to it that we speak only when speech is better than silence. Let us be swift to hear, but slow to speak, as St James puts it. Those who are always talking do very little listening.

" We should speak little with men, and much with God," observes St Alphonsus Rodriguez. " We should have God ever-present in the depths of our hearts, and make there a sort of retreat. . . . We should do or say nothing without having consulted him."

Do not say that this advice is given by a saint to saints, and by a religious to religious. You are wrong. This advice holds good for everyone, and above all for those who are not protected against attacks from without by the silence of the cloister.

" We get a false idea of the supernatural life. For my part, a Christian life is summed up in fidelity to this maxim: To live every moment of our life with Christ Jesus; to know that he, the friend, the confidant, and the Master, is always by our side, and *within* us."

These are the words of a barrister, who is president of the *Jeunesse Catholique*. Nor has the director of one of our great institutions any different advice to offer: " Everyone cannot live in the cloister, or receive the priesthood. Nevertheless, each one of us should lead an interior life, a life of grace, a divine life."

For those souls whose occupation in the world prevents them from the practice of *recollection*, he recommends the *Imitation :* " The teaching of the *Imitation* remains, indeed, the true Catholic doctrine of sacrifice, and of a life spent near to God. Catholics of to-day are not dispensed from practising this life, out-of-date as it may seem to some, and impracticable to others."*

The more intense is the life we lead in the world, the more necessary it is that we should withdraw within ourselves.

" If thou wouldst taste the sweetness of the Spirit, withdraw to a distance, where thou mayst converse freely with me."

" Be sure thou hast done naught for God, so long as thou hast not learnt how sweet it is to be alone with me."

" Do not say: I cannot recollect myself. I have not the time. If it were so, there would be all the more reason why thou shouldst isolate thyself, and take thy rest for a while."†

* E. Montier: *La Culture catholique*, 1913, ch. iv, p. 61.
† Père Gabriel Palau: *Catholique d'Action*, trans. Lebessou-Jury (Casterman). Père de Ravignan used to say: " The days on which I am overwhelmed with work, and do not know where to begin, I first of all make an extra half-hour's meditation."

This is no impossibly high ideal. In his panegyric on Pierre de Morel, a young soldier killed in the war, M. Maze-Sencier described him as one of those profound persons who know how "to recollect themselves, to search their souls, to examine themselves, and to find themselves."

" To listen to the voice of God within me, and to conform myself to its message without delay." Such was the rule of life this young soldier adopted, making his own those words of St Paul: *Gratia Dei urget nos*—the grace of God urges us—and remembering that the waters of eternal life act upon the soul in the same way as the waters of a canal press against a lock, and that it depends on us, and on our efforts, to open the gate and allow the torrent to inundate our souls. He took endless precautions, too, not to let slip a single occasion of grace, and we see from the rules he drew up that he made use of a number of conventional signs, to remind him to raise his heart frequently towards God.

The Master of our souls dwells with us continually by grace; but he only reveals his presence to those who seek him, and are in the right dispositions to find him. For he is always present, but always hidden. In order to bear this thought in mind, Pierre de Morel made use of a whole set of reminders, which together formed a sort of memorizing apparatus.

The tragic events of the war have made the necessity for leading an interior life even more obvious. " In order to revive, France must first of all collect her thoughts. How many do I call in the depths of their hearts, yet they pay no heed to my call."*

Neither weapons of war, nor (still less) talk, will bring about the salvation of the world, but " the

* *Journal spirituel de Lucie Christine*, edited by P. Poulain, p. 85.

descent of God in the midst of his creatures, for the sanctification of the individual—this, by multiplying the number of the elect, is what will prove the salvation of the nations."*

No one has pointed out more clearly than Elisabeth Leseur how we can solve, in a practical manner, the difficulty of reconciling an active exterior life with an intense interior life.

She is well aware that it is no easy task: " To keep the door of my soul ever ajar for the souls who wish to confide in me; but never to throw it wide open—to keep my innermost self always in reserve for God alone. . . . To make myself approachable . . . and at the same time to secure myself as many moments as possible for meditation, in order to give my soul the food which makes it stronger, calmer, and more filled with supernatural life."

Our first apostleship, therefore, should be that of example—by practising the habit of recollection: " There are about me many souls whom I love profoundly, and I have a great work to do for them. . . . They should be able to catch a glimpse in me of the beloved Guest of my soul. . . . Everything about me should speak of him. . . . I will not be a spiritual gossip [what a wise resolution that is !], and except when charity makes it my duty to speak, I will keep the secret of my soul, this communion alone with God, which is the guardian of strength and interior virility. We must squander nothing, not even our souls [no, indeed—above all, not our souls !], but concentrate entirely on God, in order that the rays of our soul may spread more and more around us."

Here, then, we have the rule: to cherish God within our secret soul first of all; and afterwards

* Mgr. Monestès in his letter of approbation of the *Souvenirs de Sœur Elisabeth.*

to share him with others. Unfortunately, too many of us reverse the order !*

How many of us could accuse ourselves, as Cardinal du Perron did on his death-bed, of having spent our lives rather in striving to perfect our brains by study, than to perfect our wills by the practice of an interior life.

Elisabeth Leseur gives us another golden rule in these words: " Only to give as much of ourselves as it will benefit others to receive. To keep the rest in the depths of our souls, as jealously as a miser keeps his treasure, but with the intention of sacrificing it, and giving it, when the time comes."

" In short," she observes, after making a Retreat, " to reserve for God alone the inmost recesses of my soul, and my interior Christian life; and to give to others serenity, charm, kindness, and help, in word and in deed."

Moreover, when we give of ourselves to others, we should be careful to leave God as little as possible, for this is the best way to give God to others: " To make Christ ever loving and present in our midst, the model of our lives, and the friend of every hour, whether of suffering or of happiness. To ask him to grant that he may be loved by other souls, through us, and to be (to use a favourite comparison of mine) the rude vessel which holds the bright flame, and through which this flame sheds light and heat to all around."

This doctrine is, indeed, none other than that taught by all masters of the spiritual life.

" Follow," says Père Nouet,† " the example of

---

* See on this subject the profound words of Dom Chantard, in his *Ame de tout Apostolat*, which deals with the question of work which is not founded on an interior life.

† *La Grandeur du Chrétien dans ses Rapports avec la Trinité*, p. 236.

the Eternal Father, who contemplates himself continually in his Word, and sends it into the world in such a manner that at the same time he keeps it in his breast. Your Word is the contemplation of God in you, and you in God, which you should never abandon. If you allow it to spread sometimes to other objects, you should recall it at once. If it should happen to stray, you must never allow it to become separated from you. Its progress should never be an outgoing, or, if it is, it should never be without your company."

St Francis de Sales uses the following comparisons, in order to bring home the same truth:

"A man who has received a beautiful china vessel filled with precious liquid bears it home with great care. He glances neither to the right nor to the left, but he looks now where he is going, for fear lest he should stumble and fall, and now at his burden, to see if he is holding it straight. You should do the same when you have finished your spiritual exercises. Do not unbend your mind all at once, but simply look before you. If you must needs meet someone to whom you are obliged to talk, or listen, there is no help for it. You must make the best of it, but in such a way that you can still keep watch over your heart, that the precious liquid of prayer may not be spoilt more than can be helped."

These words are to be found in the *Introduction to a Devout Life*. In the sixth book of his *Love of God* (chap. x) he writes:

"Like the child who lifts his head from his mother's breast to observe his toes, and then immediately lays it back, like the little rogue he is, so should we, as soon as we find that our attention is distracted by curiosity from our spiritual exercises, give back our hearts to the sweet contemplation of the presence of God, from which our thoughts have been distracted."

To certain privileged souls God grants special graces.

We read that when she was on her travels St Teresa never for a moment lost sight of her divine Guest. She cherished, in the inmost depths of her heart, the three Persons of the Holy Trinity, and was marvellously aware of their presence which continually accompanied her. Yet she never had a moment to herself, but was obliged, against her inclination, constantly to talk to numbers of people.

There we see the difference between the saints and ourselves!* We read, too, in the lives of certain very interior persons that as a recompense no doubt for their good-will, and their desire to lead an interior life, God has been pleased to grant them, even in the most unfavourable circumstances, an extraordinary facility for recollection.

St Margaret Mary was specially aware of the divine presence in the refectory, even during the reading. It was at a ball that Emilie d'Oultremont, the foundress of the Marie-Réparatrice nuns, heard our Lord calling her, and took the irrevocable resolution: " Master, my life shall be yours alone."

* In the Seventh Habitation of her *Interior Castle*, she thus describes the workings of the adorable Trinity within her: " God having introduced the soul into his own dwelling . . . the Three Persons of the Holy Trinity hold communication with her, speaking with her, and disclosing to her the meaning of the words of our Lord in the gospel: *If any man love me, he will keep my commandments, and my Father will love him, and we will come to him, and we will make in him our dwelling.* O my God, how many there are who are far from being struck by these words, from even noticing them, or from understanding the truth in the way I have said! Since this soul of mine has received this favour she is day by day more astonished, for it seems to her that these three divine Persons have never left her. She sees clearly that they are in the interior of her soul, in her inmost soul, and as it were in a great abyss. Such a person cannot describe this abyss, in which she feels within her the divine company."

Théodeline Dubouché, foundress of the *Institut de l'Adoration réparatrice*, found herself obliged one day to go to the opera. Yet, during the whole performance, she remained united with the presence of God.

Such special privileges as these, however, are not for you and me; nor does the doctrine of the divine Indwelling necessarily involve anything of this sort.

If, therefore, we give ourselves up to distractions, we must not expect God to remind us of his presence. But in the midst of whatever turmoil and bustle we may have to find ourselves, we can always imitate the little strolling player who went on her knees in her tent, behind the scenes, after having made her Communion, and prayed: " Lord Jesus, I do not forget that thou art within me."*

With a little effort we shall get into the habit of taking advantage of every opportunity, even the least favourable, to withdraw within ourselves.

As far as my relations with those about me are concerned, there are three rules which should be observed. I should speak with discretion—for *I* am a tabernacle. I should speak with sincerity— for he *to whom* I am speaking is also a tabernacle— or, at least, he is destined by God to be such. I should speak with charity—for he *of whom* I am speaking is—or can be—also a tabernacle.†

* Certain ejaculatory prayers are very helpful: *Dominus tecum !* . . . *Per ipsum, cum ipso, in ipso* (by him, with him, in him), and how many more !

† Those who really have the faith will spontaneously form these habits of charity and good manners towards others. St Aloysius was frequently obliged by his superiors to restrain the marks of honour he showed his companions. M. Olier used to genuflect when he passed by the cell of Père de Condren, his second superior after Cardinal de Bérulle, and when asked why he did so, he replied: " It is not Père de Condren who is there, but God who dwells within Père de Condren."

If it is the spirit of apostleship that bids us go forth, in order to save souls, we should be all the more anxious to avoid losing sight of God. When the priest says Mass, he turns to the faithful several times to remind them that God is with them. *Dominus vobiscum.* May we not venture to suggest that he ought, several times during the day, to turn and address these words to his own soul—*Dominus tecum ?*

" To attain the perfection of spiritual life," writes Sister Elizabeth of the Trinity, worthy daughter of the holy mother St Teresa, " we must live in the supernatural, realize that God is near within us; and set out to do everything *with Him.* Then we are never commonplace, even in our most ordinary actions; for we are not wrapped up in these things, but remain above them. The supernatural soul has no dealings with second causes, but only with God."

" When we are busy," she adds, " and seem to emulate Martha, our souls may still dwell wrapped, like Mary, in contemplation, drinking thirstily of the waters of eternal life. This is how I understand the apostolate."*

If this conception of the apostolate comes more easily to a cloistered nun, yet it is far from being beyond the reach of any one of us. Without it, no work for souls which we undertake, however much fame may be ours, will bear good fruit.

* The writings of St Teresa are studded with similar thoughts. On one page, taken at random, we read: " You might think that when necessary occupations drag you out from the interior retreat of your heart, you are guilty of a great breach of recollection. You are mistaken. Provided that afterwards you faithfully return to it, the divine Master will make everything contribute to benefit your soul. When the action has interrupted contemplation, there is no other remedy but to turn once more to contemplation (*Interior Castle*, Second Habitation, ch. i). See also, in particular, *The Way of Perfection*, ch. xxix and xxx.

" You are a temple," says Mgr. Gay, shrewdly;
" put things in the porch, men in the nave—but
keep the sanctuary for God."

CHAPTER III

TO CONQUER OUR TREASURE

THE defensive has never been the favourite tactic
of nations—or of souls—whose minds are bent on
victory.

It is not enough simply to protect or defend the
interior castle of our souls, wherein God dwells.
In order that this castle should be really our own
we must conquer it, and often at the cost of a bitter
and prolonged struggle.

Even were the masters of the spiritual life not
unanimous on this point, the most elementary
personal experience will be sufficient to prove to us
that we shall only find God on the condition that
we are prepared to lose ourselves.

Let no one imagine, therefore, that the journey
from the exterior to the interior life can be made in a
sleeping-car, on velvet cushions.   No, indeed.   We
have but to open the *Imitation*, the *Spiritual Combat*,
the *Exercises* of St Ignatius, the works of St Teresa,
or St Francis de Sales, or any other reliable ascetical
writer, to find the same phrases constantly recur-
ring.   It is always a question of overcoming ourselves, of withstanding our caprices, of waging
war, and of sacrifice, *agere contra, ut homo vincat
seipsum.* All this means war, and the spiritual
book which is not *war-like* is no book of solid
piety.

Many people, however, when they realize the
absolute necessity for this war on themselves, are

discouraged, and begin to stumble, and to hesitate.
Right at the beginning they read that they must
" overcome themselves," and they are terrified.
" To overcome themselves." Then, they say, that
means fighting against themselves, risking something, in fact ? And if I am overcome, even by
myself, shall I not be less than I was before—like
France without Alsace-Lorraine, deprived of just
what I hold most dear ?

It might possibly be better, in order to attract
souls, to show them first of all the interior of the
castle, that they may be dazzled by the wealth
which may be theirs, and then, afterwards, on the
way out, let them see the ravaging words which are
engraved over the threshold.

It is just a question of method, but not without
importance, perhaps. I need a screen between
suffering and my fear—and that screen is love. I
need something to hide the wood of the sacrifice from
my shrinking eyes—and I have our Lord. I need
to be assured that my efforts, and the sacrifices
which I shall probably be called upon deliberately
and of set purpose to make will be rewarded—and
that reward will be intimacy with God. Then—I
am ready ! With my eyes fixed firmly on the end
I have in view I shall fight, even to the end. I know
what is at stake. I am fighting for the possession
of that kingdom within which is mine, and in which
God himself is pleased to dwell.

Three stages will mark the history of my conquest. My first task will be to find myself, to obtain
full possession of myself.

I must then realize that I am not alone—that
persons dwell within my soul—the divine Guest and
myself.

Finally, I must realize that of the two, one is in the
way. Hence I shall strive to make myself as small

as possible, in order to lease the whole kingdom of my soul to God alone.

These, then, are the three stages:

    (1) Myself alone;
    (2) He and I;
    (3) He alone.

MYSELF ALONE

At first sight it may seem that to "withdraw within oneself" is a very simple business. What man but, after the turmoil of the day, desires to return to the peace of his own home?

To his own home, yes—but to his own soul, that is not so certain!

When our Lord walked through the streets of Jericho, and invited Zacheus to return to his house that he might receive him as his guest, where was Zacheus, and what was he doing?

Zacheus had climbed up into a sycamore tree, that he might see better. Like him we, too, have left our homes, and have climbed to some point of observation whence we can look down and lose nothing of the spectacle of the crowd, of the movement and of the noise around us.

If Zacheus climbed his tree, however, it was for the good reason that he was anxious to see Christ. Is that our purpose, too, or have we been simply attracted by the changing sights and scenes of the street below?

"Zacheus," says our Lord, "make haste and come down!"

To us, too, he addresses the same invitation. For the agile Jew it was an easy matter to obey our Lord's commands—to climb down from his sycamore. In our case, however, it is not so simple.

"Hodie in domo tua oportet me manere. This day I must abide in thy house. Come down, and *return*

to thy house without delay. Presently, this very day, thou wilt receive my visit. See that thou art not missing. See that I find thee there."

From top to bottom of the tree, and thence to his house. That is the journey Zacheus has to take. It is no great distance. In our case, however, the journey is longer.

Zacheus will meet many people on the way home. Friends will want to stop him, to distract his attention, to interest him, delay him, amuse him. The *useless* is always so attractive! In order to sacrifice it, we need great courage. We have but to read the lives of the saints in order to realize this.

While reading the Psalms one day, St Pambo suddenly realized that God does not dwell with those whose minds are occupied with worldly things. "It is enough," he cries. "I will first put this lesson into practice, and when I have learnt it I will return to hear the rest." At the end of forty-nine years spent in the desert, he is asked if he has not yet learnt the lesson. And he answers: "Not yet!"

It was the voice of humility that spoke—the voice of a man who has measured his task, and has no illusions on the subject.

Those who do not realize the difficulties of such a task have but to open at random the pages of the first three books of the *Imitation*, or the precious tract of Blessed Albert the Great, *On Union with God*. There is but one road which leads to contemplation—the road called Renunciation. Let no one imagine that it is a question of Quietism—of passive and blissful rest in God. It is a hundred miles removed from anything of the sort.

We need scarcely insist further on this point, for it must be clear, from what we have already said on this subject, that the souls who have learned contemplation have done so at the cost of complete surrender of themselves.

The road which leads to the Kingdom Within is littered with the remains of the idols which stood in the way, and had to be destroyed. A few passers-by stand at the cross-ways. They are, says St Augustine, the passions and the caprices which have not succeeded in hindering our path, for we have put them to flight.

Yes, it is a triumphal way—but God alone knows at what cost the triumph has been won !

HE AND I

Mortification is equally essential at this second stage. The soul which is in a state of grace, and which manages to find itself, finds God also. Its device is no longer *Myself Alone*, but—*We Two*. At the same time we carry about with us a number of other things—which, when we come to examine them, turn out to be so many incumbrances.

Hence it comes about that, in the case of the greater number of souls, that happens which once happened at Bethlehem. " There was no room for them in the inn." And these things which cumber the ground of the inn which is our soul—what mole-hills they are, and what mountains we make of them ! They fill up every corner, and when God comes, as he came to Bethlehem, and knocks at our door, " there is no room in the inn."*

* The vibrating words of E. Hello in his *Physionomies de Saints* on this theme—" there is no room in the inn "—are well known:

" The history of the world is summed up in these three words; and this history, so abridged, so substantial, is not read. For to read is to understand. And eternity will not be too long in which to take and measure what is written in these words: *No room in the inn*. There was room enough for other travellers. There was no room for these. What was given to all was refused to Mary and Joseph; and in a

Our souls, which we throw open to all and sundry, which are the meeting-place of so many, have no room for God. Or if, by the fact that we are not in mortal sin, God does, indeed, dwell with us, it is as if, in most cases, he were not there, for we ignore his presence, and pay no heed to it.

And the divine Guest, banished to a dim and dusty corner, in disgrace, is waiting until we can find time to attend to him. Too often he will wait in vain, and one day his silent supplication will turn into words of condemnation: *Hospes eram, et non collegistis me. Esurivi, et non dedistis mihi manducare. Sitivi, et non dedistis mihi potum.* I was thy guest, and—for want of recollection—thou didst not receive me. I hungered to give myself to thee. I desired with a desire which has not ceased since the night of Holy Thursday to eat the Pasch with thee, and thou didst not respond. Thou didst pay no heed to my hunger. Thou didst not invite me to thy table. I thirsted for the love I saw thee squandering on creatures—on so many wretched,

---

few minutes Jesus Christ was to be born! The expected one of nations knocks at the door of the world, and there was no room for him in the inn! The Roman Pantheon, that inn for idols, found room for thirty thousand demons, taking names which were thought to be divine. But Rome found no place for Jesus Christ in her Pantheon. One would be inclined to say that she guessed that Jesus Christ would have none of that place, and that company. The more insignificant one is, the more easily one finds a place. He who bears on him a human treasure has more difficulty in finding a place. He who bears something marvellous and god-like has still more difficulty. He who bears God finds no room. It seems as if people guess that he will need too much room, and that, however small he makes himself, he cannot overcome the instinct of those who repulse him. He cannot succeed in persuading them that he is like other men. In vain he hides his grandeur, it bursts forth in spite of him, and, instinctively, at his approach, doors are shut. . . ."

and often unworthy, creatures, in any case less lovely than I, who am the Creator, and Love itself.   And thou didst laugh at my thirst, or ignore it.   I thirsted to see thee break with some of thy comforts, of thy caprices, of those useless trifles which were taking possession of thy soul, sowing discord there, so that I, the Essential, might reign supreme in thine unburdened soul.   And thou hast seen nothing, understood nothing, or, at least, desired nothing.   I admit that it is painful to renounce the fragment for the whole.   Yet thou dost not lack the gift of reason.   Art thou not "naturalized divine"? Very well, then. . . .

Every man who would be a follower of Christ must take up his cross and deny himself.   How much more is required of the soul which aspires to perfection in the spiritual life !

The grace which we receive at our baptism endows us, not with the fulness, but with the germ of our supernatural life.   It is God himself whom we receive, but the manner in which we receive him is limited in proportion to our individual capacity.

This germ develops under the action of the Holy Ghost, with the co-operation of the soul, which "by the same spirit" must mortify "the works of the flesh."

St Paul observes truly that at our baptism we receive only the pledges of eternal life.   This explains how the possession of God may be restricted in the case of certain souls, and, consequently, how we can constantly enlarge our capacity to contain God in our hearts, if we allow Christ, who has freed us once for all from the bondage of sin, by his blood, to liberate us more and more by our fidelity to his invitations.

After having, without any help of theirs, saved

all men in his Person, he sanctifies each one in proportion as he will correspond, by his Spirit.

This explains the ardent desire of the saints.

" As long as God gives me life," writes Pauline Reynolds, during her Retreat in 1902, " I wish to grow in love, in union, in capacity to possess God for all eternity.   Death will fix me in the state in which I shall find myself.   How many opportunities to glorify God, how many occasions of merit I have neglected !   This is perhaps the last effort of his mercy. . . ."

He who opens the gates of his soul to receive the waters of grace will grow in grace.   He will be swept away by its tide.   The life of " the Three " will increase within him, like a vessel which increases with its contents, and is ever full.

" There is none save me and thee," said our Lord to one of his saints.   In order that this may be true of us, how much detachment we must learn !   What complete self-surrender will be necessary, if that motto of Sister Elizabeth's—" Alone with the One " —is to become, not a mere formula, but a vivid reality.

" Let there be no go-between between God and your soul," was the advice of the Curé d'Ars. Only those who have tried to dispense with any " go-between " know what it has cost !

In the words of St Paul to Timothy we find the same inevitable rule: *Si commortui, et convivemus*. If we be dead, we shall live also.

GOD ALONE

The soul may make final progress, and lose sight of herself to such an extent that henceforth her sole consideration is *God Alone.*

She began by possessing herself, by "being her own"—*anima mea in manibus meis semper*. Descending within herself, she discovered that she was not alone. Now that she has found God within her, nothing—and least of all herself—has any weight with her. It is the last stage in the spiritual ascent, and the last stage of the soul's descent within herself.

A certain writer has summed it up in the epigram: "Over the edge of self we find God."

At first sight it would seem an easy task to "eliminate self."

By constant examinations of conscience the soul has been seen reflected, as in a mirror, and the soul of man is not a particularly beautiful object. Leaving on one side sin—for we are dealing now with the soul which is in a state of grace—how many ugly and shabby actions, how many mean and cowardly deeds, how many broken pledges, how many short cuts in prayer, how many barely fulfilled promises, how many wilful distractions, disfigure it !

At sight of it, we feel we want to run away, and leave it to its fate. We make up our minds to give up praying, to leave off assailing the ears of the Master by the endless repetition of the same wretchedness, the same petty meanness.

As a rule, the knowledge of all this does not vex, or even surprise us. But on certain days it becomes unbearable. We become a burden to ourselves. We feel that we would sooner talk to God on any other subject. We find ourselves so uninteresting. How can we hope to interest God in our nothingness ?

But suppose, instead of talking to him about myself, I speak only of him ? If I speak, not of my poverty, but of his riches; not of my wretchedness, but of his mercy; not of my crosses, but of his Cross; not of my feeble ambitions, but of his glory ? *Gloria in excelsis Deo.* Glory be to the Father, and to the Son, and to the Holy Ghost. *Gratias agimus tibi, propter magnam gloriam tuam.* Let me, too, emulate St Teresa, who was never tired of repeating, in transports of joy, these words from the Creed—*cujus regni non erit finis.*

However deeply we may be penetrated by such sentiments as these, we shall never succeed entirely in our efforts to eliminate self—that "fallen god who remembers the skies"; that ego wherein lurk the tiger and the ape; that self with all its blemishes, its baseness, its ingrained meanness; that indestructible self-love which, as St Francis de Sales warns us, will only become extinct a quarter of an hour after our death.

Spiritual writers, following the example of St Paul, call this self the "old man"—a paradoxical phrase enough, seeing that this singular individual stalks abroad with every sign of perennial youth !

"We are two," Joseph de Maistre used to say, "myself and . . . the other!" He spoke truly. Only the "other" is strangely united to the "self," and the story of their relations is one long story of parleys with the enemy.

"There were two of us. I have thrown one out of the window," was the humorous reply attributed to Père de Ravignan to a person who asked him to relate his experiences in the noviciate.

We can guess what sacrifices were implied in those words—sacrifices which St Augustine foresaw when he cried aloud to God: *Eia, dulcissime Deus, hoc mihi pactum erit: plane moriar mihi ipsi, ut tu solus in me vivas.* "Lord, this shall be a covenant between us: I will die entirely to myself, that you alone may dwell in me."

And M. Olier prayed thus: O All, O my All, I am no longer myself. I am no longer aught but You."

In order to be able to speak thus, what sacrifices he had imposed upon himself, even going so far as to offer himself to God, at Montmartre, as a " Victim." " I took pleasure, my God, in presenting myself before you as a victim, and in saying to you: ' O God of my heart, spare me nothing, cut me, break me, rend the victim to pieces.' "

The piety of General de Sonis is well known. His act of self-surrender was made in these terms:

" O my God, may you be blessed when you send me trials. I desire to be broken, consumed, destroyed by you. Annihilate me more and more. . . . Turn and turn me about. Destroy me, and use me. I desire to be reduced to nothing for love of you. . . . Let me be crucified—but by you !"

Another soul used to say, more briefly: " Myself equals zero !"

You see—it is no longer a question of sacrificing " the big things." The little things must go, too.

This is so obvious that a single illustration will serve our purpose.

We will take it from the first book of *The Ascent of Mount Carmel*, of St John of the Cross. The third chapter is entitled: " It is necessary that the soul should overcome even the smallest passions, in order to enter upon the divine union."

" The reason for this," explains the saint, " is that the state of divine union consists in the soul being wholly transformed into the will of God, so that the will of God may be the only beginning and the only end which will cause it to act in all things as if the will of God and the will of the soul were but one will. Now this transformation is necessary, since, without it, the soul might have a leaning towards imperfections which would be displeasing to the Lord, for it would desire those things which he did not desire."

The whole book is intended to serve as a commentary on the following programme:

To enjoy the taste of all things, have no taste for anything.

To possess all things, resolve to possess nothing.

To be all things, be willing to be nothing.

When you stop at one thing you cease to open yourself to the All.

For to come to the All you must give up the all.

And when you should have attained to owning the All, you must own it by re-desiring nothing.

For if you desire to have something in the All, you have not your treasure purely in God.

Sainte-Beuve tells us in his *Port Royal* the story of an old and saintly abbess, who, when called upon to give up her office, could not persuade herself to part with the key of a little garden to which, as abbess, she had enjoyed the right of access. How easy we all find it to keep back the key of our little garden, and what a sacrifice it means to hand it over! We are like the child who had a cupboardful of toys, and who, when asked to give some away to the poor, discovered that they were the very ones he could not spare; or that other child who said his prayers at his mother's knee, and who, when he came to the words: " My God, I offer you all I possess," added under his breath: " Except my little lamb !"

The big sacrifices are—comparatively speaking—easy to make. It is the little ones which cost us so dear !

While making her monthly retreat, at the age of twenty-three, Pauline Reynolds noticed these words written on the back of a holy picture: " If you would be perfect, let your heart cling to *nothing*. Give *all* your love to Jesus Christ."

" My memory," she writes, " went back over the many, many things which I cherished like so many priceless treasures. I decided to make a sacrifice of them. . . . I had with me some precious letters, dating from my earliest infancy. I loved them so much that I never, so to speak, parted with them. I made a parcel of them, without daring to glance at them, and I gave it to M. le Curé [her confessor] to be burnt, for I could not possibly have brought myself to do it. . . . It was an indescribable wrench. I went round my room, and took everything—letters, locks of hair, dried flowers—all were cast into the fire. It was an enormous sacrifice. *I do not think I have ever done anything which cost me so much.*"

And we see, when we read her life, that God made this " enormous sacrifice " the condition on which he bestowed on her such rare graces.

" Since that moment," she adds, " I have never felt the least attachment for any object whatsoever. I understood the divine jealousy of him who desired my heart so greatly that he could not bear that I should attach myself even to a letter or a flower."

Thérèse Durnerin, foundress of the Society of the Friends of the Poor, once received a large crucifix which had been brought back from Rome.

" Very often," relates her sister Noémie, " she saw the wound in the Heart streaming, not with blood, but with precious stones, in a chalice held by invisible hands. During the most painful years of her life, at a time when her soul was plunged into a sea of bitterness, this vision consoled her powerfully." In order to die to herself, Thérèse made the resolution to part with this crucifix, and sent it to the *Missions* with a number of other objects which were dear to her as souvenirs.*

Sometimes the " divine jealousy " of the Master will exact a still more painful sacrifice.

In order to follow her vocation, St Jeanne de

* See her *Life*, by H. M. Hamez (Lib. St Paul), p. 25.

Chantal was obliged to step over the bodies of her children, who threw themselves on the door-step. Comtesse d'Hoogvorst, Émilie d'Oultremont, had likewise to break the most precious ties, in order to become a Réparatrice nun.

The first—and the last—word of God to Moses, when he led his people to the Land of Promise is this: " *Exi*—go forth. . . . set out, cut, break "; and every soul which sets out on her pilgrimage to the stars will find that the same words will meet her eye, and more and more often, as she leaves each stage of the journey behind.

It does not matter whether it is a coil of rope or an end of string—whatever it is that holds us back, we shall never be perfectly united with God until we have thrown it off.

" It matters nothing," says St John of the Cross, in the chapter just quoted, " if the string to which we tie a bird is thick or thin, since in any case it prevents it from flying. In the same way, it matters naught if an imperfection be great or small, since in either case it hinders the soul from spreading its wings towards perfection and union with God."

That our aspirations towards such perfection and such union must be made subject to such considerations as the state of our health, our duties, and our position in life, and that we must on no account rush precipitately and without guidance towards a state of perfection which, however beautiful in itself, is out of our particular reach, it goes without saying, nor is there any necessity for us to remind the reader to exercise due prudence in this regard.

In the wise and emphatic words of St Catherine of Siena, we must give ourselves to God " with measure, and without measure."

CONCLUSION

A GREAT many people find piety where there is none. Some find it in particular attitudes and gestures. Mgr. Camus, the friend of St Francis de Sales, wishing to imitate his sanctity, was inspired to copy the way in which he held his head, rather on one side. There was no piety in that, and Mgr. Camus soon realized the fact. As a young man Henri d'Alzon made a similar mistake, and the Little Flower tells us how often a certain nun nearly caused her to give way to impatience by murmuring her prayers half-aloud by her side.

Piety does not reside in any particular attitude, and God can hear prayers which are said silently, quite as well as any others.

Other people fancy that piety consists in a multiplicity of spiritual exercises—so many rosaries, so many little "offices," so much reading of pious books. They imagine that it would be very wrong of them not to subscribe to such and such a review, and they expect the skies to fall if they are obliged to alter the time fixed for a certain devotion, or to miss it altogether. Now, such exercises of piety are certainly necessary, but they are not the whole, or even the principal part, of the spiritual life.

Others make piety a matter of sentiment, and when God sends them consolation in prayer they think it is merited, and confuse facility with virtue.

True piety is a question of *spirit*—the spirit which animates our lives. It is, above all, a matter of intelligence. In this domain, as in so many others, there is much waste of ill-directed energy. Many souls are generous, but they tend to stray aimlessly down side-tracks of piety, simply for want of a simple, broad, comprehensive and precise guiding principle.

Piety, as we understand it, is essentially *steadfast*. It is founded on dogma, and in particular on that central dogma round which all others revolve. Thus, firmly rooted piety will be sustained by a simple and traditional rule of life. It will be based, not on sentiment, but on faith. It will demand—and inspire —great energy, and even, in certain cases, the complete sacrifice of self.

Piety which is based on one of the fundamental dogmas of our faith, and the normal method of which is that of renunciation, is *steadfast* piety.

True piety will also be *profound*.

It will penetrate the inmost recesses of our souls. It will make known to us royal secrets.

He who lives with God in his soul, and by God within him, can scarcely bring himself to act superficially, without stability or serious purpose. No. Those whose life spreads from within outwards, and back again, will not suffer from that terrible want of concentration which is the blemish of commonplace, gushing natures. Their spiritual life will be reduced to *unity*.

How many souls take up one pious practice after another, without making the slightest attempt to link up one with the other, to form a chain which will guide them through the mazes of the spiritual life. Such people are constantly changing their tactics, because no particular line of conduct seemed to be marked out for them. Their spiritual life lacks a guiding principle. They are at the mercy of a book, or a popular devotion. They have no dominant idea round which their whole existence may crystallize.

The doctrine of the divine Indwelling is, above

all, calculated to provide such a link; for the chief and, indeed, the whole—problem of our existence is surely none other than this—our sanctification.

This piety is of an *expanding* nature. It is not concentrated on some narrow issue. It will enable the soul to embrace the broadest and most beautiful ideas of spiritual values. Seen by the light of God's presence within us, all things will be made clear to us, and we shall arrive at *intelligence*, in the literal sense of the word: *intus legere*. We shall learn to read wonderful and unsuspected secrets in the book of our soul—and we shall discover, at last, that only the *inner meaning* of things has any significance to us whatsoever. In the midst of all the events which take place around us, we shall seek behind the *historical fact* for the divine purpose which lies hidden from the eyes of most of our fellows. The men among whom we are thrown will seem puny creatures in comparison with the God who dwells—or desires to dwell—within our hearts. We shall understand, in short, that only one thing really matters: the life of God within our souls. We shall know that when the work of sanctification has been accomplished within the soul of the last of God's elect, the world itself will be no more.

The remembrance that God is our Guest will also expand the soul, because of the constant efforts which the soul will make to grow and increase, in order to make more room for his presence.

" It is necessary that he should increase, and that I should decrease," said St John the Baptist. In the sacred Humanity of our Lord the divinity was perfect from the beginning. In us, the " other Christs," the divine life is susceptible of increase. By origin we are, as the Fathers put it, " budding gods," destined to come to flower. At first we possess but the beginning of his substance—*initium*

substantiae ejus (Heb. iii 14). It rests with us to
strive *to grow into the increase of God* (Col. ii 19).

It follows naturally that piety such as this will
be dynamic—that it will constantly stimulate our
hearts and minds. *Ecce non dormitabit neque dormiet
qui custodit Israel*. He that watcheth over Israel
slumbers not, nor sleeps.

"Christ," says St Augustine, "is in the centre
of our souls, and thence he sees what our hand
does, what our tongue says, what our mind is thinking, and what are our inmost feelings. With what
vigilance, what piety, and what chastity we should
live, seeing that we are ever under the eye of this
most holy Master.*

And St Anselm adds: "Has not the Apostle declared, O Christian, that thou art the very body of
Christ? Guard, then, both this body and its
members with all the honour which is their due.
Thine eyes are the eyes of Christ. Wilt thou turn the
eyes of Christ, who is truth itself, on the things of
vanity? Thy lips are the lips of Christ. Wilt thou
open them, I do not say to calumny and wicked
words, but even to useless discourses, to frivolous
conversations? With what vigilance and what
respect should we govern all our senses, and all the
members of our body, since the Lord in person rules
them, possesses them, and presides over their
actions."†

What can be better calculated to inspire zeal
than such a thought as this?

The spectacle of Christ banished on every side,
and knocking in vain at the door of men's souls, is
heartrending. *Quid hic agis, Elia?* What dost
thou here, Elias? we ask ourselves. Others are
fighting the good fight, and wilt thou remain here
idle? Wilt thou not go forth, as John the Baptist

---

* *De Ascens.*, Sermon xi.   † *Meditation*, i.

went forth to the multitudes on the banks of the Jordan, and cry out in their midst: "There is one in the midst of you, whom you know not"?

"Is it enough," asks Pauline Reynolds, "that I should know you and love you? Ah, no. Jesus, my Lord, manifest yourself to the world, to all! Grant that your friends, and those who are consecrated to your service, may know you indeed, and make others know you. Make known to souls the attractions of your holy mysteries. Let all your followers have a holy thirst for all you have to give, and let them give of what they have received in order to draw souls, minds, and hearts to you. And then, O Jesus, then, O God, there are the many millions who know you not at all—for whom your Incarnation, your Mysteries, your Gospel, and your Church are a dead letter. Have pity on them, have pity. Show yourself to the world."*

True piety is *joyful*. We should have but one cause for sadness—that we are not saints. How many of us would be better able to bear the troubles of life, if we did but realize that in very truth we are —or should be—*God-bearers*, for God dwells within us, by sanctifying grace.

We may lose our all. If God remains, what more can we want? We may be abandoned by all. If God does not abandon us, we shall miss very little. Alone with God, we are in the majority. Alone with him, our solitude is as richly peopled as we can possibly desire.

In short, when St Paul tells us to rejoice, what else does he mean, except just this: that we should always be in a state of grace?

"There is a joy," writes Elizabeth Leseur, in her *Journal*, "which the worst sorrows cannot destroy;

* Vol. II, ch. ii, Med. 14.

a light which shines through the deepest gloom; a power which sustains our every weakness. Alone, we should fall to the ground, as Christ fell when he carried his cross. Yet we go marching on. Our falls are but of a moment. We are soon up again, full of courage. *For we can do all in him who strengtheneth us.* Feeble creatures that we are, we carry within us Infinite Strength, and in the depths of our souls there shines the Light which will never fail. How can we fail, then, to rejoice, in spite of all, with supernatural joy, when we possess God for life and for all eternity ?"

True piety makes us *free*.

Besides being cowardly, how inconsistent is human respect ! We find the good blushing at their goodness, and the wicked taking pride in their wickedness. To lead a good life is a crime ! To lead a bad one, a matter for glory ! What a source of satisfaction to the devil, and what a disgrace to mankind is this barbarous reversal of values ! Who is it who dwells within the soul of the passer-by who is pleased to jeer at me, because I am on my way to Mass and Holy Communion ? Yet I, within whose soul God dwells, blush, hide myself, and feel ashamed.

Human respect is nothing more than contempt for the divine. It is as if the dead were to sneer at the living, and the living to dread the smiles of the dead !

Agnosce, o christiane, dignitatem tuam. Recognize thy grandeur, and learn to be free, St Leo, Pope, used to say. " Thou who art the Son of God, the King's Son, dost thou pay heed to the son of a slave ? Lift up thine head. Go forward. Hold thine head high. If any must needs blush, and seek to hide himself, it is not thou. Learn this, and never forget it."

It is a topsy-turvy world we live in.* Let it be ours to set it on all-fours once again. There is nothing to be ashamed of in preserving our chastity, in leading a life of prayer, in being a *God-bearer*. To betray one's faith, on the contrary, to forget heaven, to fall into sin—that deserves our shame. Be sure of this, and, when necessary, preach it on the house-tops.

There must be no contempt for others, mind; no pride in yourself. What that man is, but for God's grace, you might have been. What you are now, you will only continue to be by the help of the same grace. Avoid pride, therefore, but be immensely confident. You are in a state of grace. You are a God-bearer—and how much that means !

" It may be," wrote Hello, " that vanity would become almost impossible if men had any idea of their greatness. The voice of glory would stifle within them the small voice of self-love. It is God's desire that we should share his life. He, the Infinite, desires to give himself to you, and he forbids you, great as you are, to be content with anything less. He tells you the price of your redemption, in order that you may know your own worth. He ordains for you joys, the splendour of which you must learn to grasp—and you, young man, who are brother to St John, your wildest ambition is to imitate some imbecile or other who has spent twenty years talking to no effect—if not worse !"

True piety takes the Blessed Virgin for its model. At the beginning of these pages our thoughts

* " For a reason as mysterious as it is significant, it happens that he who desires to lead an honest and regular life is almost always in bad odour with his old companions, in whose eyes it is more contemptible to be converted than to commit a forgery." (Jörgensen: *St Catherine of Siena and her Disciples.* Revue des Jeunes, November 25, 1917.)

turned naturally towards our Blessed Lady. It is
also natural that, at the close of our task, we should
turn to her again. It is said that M. Olier often
heard a voice which said: " I desire that thou
shouldst dwell in ceaseless contemplation." In
Mary's case, no such invitation was needed. Even
before the Annunciation, what a fulness of divine
life she enjoyed ! If the great duty of every thinking
Christian, who is enlightened by the divine Treasure
he bears within his breast, is to let himself be " invaded
by the Three," how ardent must have been this
desire in the case of our Lady, who was so well
instructed in the divine mysteries, and who, as the
Church tells us, was " full of grace " from the
moment of her birth.

Spiritus Sanctus superveniet in te. The Holy
Ghost, said the angel Gabriel, shall come upon thee.
Already, by grace, he dwells within Mary's soul,
together with the Father and the Word. But God
will descend in a miraculous manner within her,
and divine life in her will be intensified to the highest
possible degree. Already she is *gratia plena.* What
could be more ? Can we say that she is now *super-
plena*—overflowing ? Henceforth, until Christmas
night, she will bear within her breast the sacred
Humanity of our Lord. How greatly will this
treasure enrich her ! Yet, when all is said and done,
that which most of all enriches her is not so much
the human advent of the Son of God as the divine
advent of the Holy Ghost, which has made it possible.
Our Lady's chief ornament now is not so much the
presence of the Man-God within her; not so much
the matchless mystery of her maternity; as the
divine Indwelling within her soul, by virtue of
which she has been chosen to be the mother of
God.

Let us pass on now to the day of Pentecost.
During the whole of our Lord's life upon earth

Mary was ever by his side, growing in grace, following the example, the counsel, and the life of her Son. Then the day comes when Jesus is called upon to leave her, and to return to his Father. Henceforth Mary will enjoy only as much of his sacred Humanity as we may all share—his presence under the appearances of bread and wine.

But the Holy Ghost will descend upon the Apostles, and through them upon the world. This coming, too, this extraordinary gift Mary, the queen of Apostles, will share with them, in the Cenacle.

"Give place to the Holy Spirit, the Paraclete," says the priest to the demon, each time he administers the sacrament of baptism. When the heart is already free, and not only free but filled with God, as Mary's was, what must have been the effect within it on this third "Invasion" of the Spirit, at the moment of Pentecost?

Our Lady's chief adornment is not so much the mission she was called upon to fulfil, as her heart. And so it is with us. What alone really matters is not our outward actions, or our mission in life, but the divine life within our hearts. *Deus intuetur cor.* God reads our hearts. That is all he cares about. He sees, in a glance, if there is room for him there, and how much room we will give him. *Deus qui in corde beatae Mariae dignum Filio tuo habitaculum praeparasti*, says the holy liturgy. God prepared himself a worthy dwelling for his Son, in our Lady's heart.

We must now ask ourselves: is my soul, or is it not, the abode of the Son of God? If it is, to what a degree, and what effect does it have on my life?

Man may take an interest in a hundred other matters. Apart from this matter the world has no interest at all for God. Would that we might follow his example in this respect!

Pentecost having been accomplished, Mary dwelt in the house of St John.

Her divine Child has left her; but divine life is still hers, and her whole existence is spent in silent communion with the divine Guests of her soul. Her life is uneventful, save for the apostles' Mass every morning, " the greatest event in the history of mankind . . . the repetition of the decisive hour when our sinful and justly-disinherited earth journeyed suddenly forth towards the fulness of supernatural life."*

" I have no work outside this," said Ruysbroeck; and our Lady might say the same.

This, too, should be true of all of us who aspire to a truly Christian life: we should live, not an exterior, but an *interior* life.

We should be glad indeed if any souls, after reading these pages, should feel a desire to live no longer " outside," but " inside "—to turn their thoughts into their own souls, where he—the Holy Trinity, Father, Son, and Holy Ghost—lies hidden.

" How many souls will one day utter a cry of surprise at the discovery of that *inner life* which is theirs, and of which they have hitherto been unaware !"

When our eyes first fell on these words of Mgr. D'Hulst we were filled with sorrow. It seemed to us that we could not resign ourselves to such a state of affairs; and we determined, in spite of more than one obstacle, to endeavour to remedy it, knowing full well that, however inadequate these pages might prove, the Master who speaks to us from the depths of our souls would supply what was wanting, and that thus these words of ours would bear fruit, even

* G. Goyau, in a review of *Lettres des Prêtres aux Armées'* by V. Bucailla.

if no more than one single soul should respond to their appeal.

" A soul is a quite big enough diocese," St Francis de Sales used to say. What a reward would be ours if but one Christian man or woman were to resolve that, for the future, the Indwelling of the Holy Ghost within our souls should be no dead letter, and to determine to live, from that day forth, *an interior life !*